WRITE YOUR BOOK IN A FLASH

THE PAINT-BY-NUMBERS SYSTEM TO WRITE
THE BOOK OF YOUR DREAMS—FAST!

DAN JANAL

ISBN: 978-1-63161-048-6

Published by TCK Publishing

www.TCKPublishing.com

Get discounts and special deals on our best-selling books at

www.TCKPublishing.com/bookdeals

DEDICATION

To Susan Tracy

CONTENTS

PRAISE FOR *FLASH*

"What a treat! It is excellent. Your style of writing is easy and *filled* with many practical, useful points. This is a great blueprint with many practical, actionable items for writing my next book."

—Louise Griffith, author, *One Shining Light*

"There is so much in this book that is helpful. I have enjoyed the exercises, as well—a great, brain-friendly guide."

—Stephen Moulton, author, *The CEO's Advantage,*
   7 Keys for Hiring Extraordinary Leaders

"What a great book! You will help thousands of people release their voices onto the page."

—Margo O'Dell, president, MAO Consulting

"I wish I'd had this book when I wrote my first book. It would have shortened my writing time by several months! Dan knows what he's talking about. Really. Just buy this book, read it, and follow Dan's brilliant Paint-by-Numbers System."

—Greg Godek, author and publisher, *1001 Ways to be Romantic*—
   A 3.1-million-copy bestseller

"Dan Janal's superpower is to bring order out of chaos. Anyone thinking about writing a book or a next book needs this book to shortcut without compromising quality."

—Cathy Paper, president, Rock Paper Star

"I've been 75 percent done with my book after three years of work. I bet I'll have it done in a month."

—David Goldman, The Laughing Stockbroker

"Beta reading a book outside my genre turned out to be very exciting. I can't believe the knowledge I gained, and I had to keep myself from filling in the blanks on the pages. It really gets your wheels turning to write your book...or hire Dan Janal. It will be very tempting to get him involved in your masterpiece, just to get it right."

—Rhonda Gilliland, author and editor, Cooked to Death series

"I have the attention span of a gnat, so reading a whole book in a day isn't something I have done in years! Most books don't keep my attention for a variety of reasons. You did! Generally easy to read and engaging. Lots of great tips on how to actually make it happen. Many times, in books like these I come across something I haven't done before, and I walk away frustrated because I understand what needs to happen but don't know how to do it. You have a straightforward way of walking through each part that I can see would get me to the finish line. Overall, loved it!"

—Heidi Pozzo, founder, Pozzo Consulting

"*Write Your Book in a Flash!* has great material for anyone who is interested in writing a book. I am writing my second book, and Dan's information has given me a whole new perspective on my writing. It would have been nice to have this book five years ago when I was doing my first one."

—Rob Oliver, author, *Still Walking*

"Dan's experience and wisdom has made all the difference, helping me take my book idea from a 'someday' project to words on a page! Yes, this is a book I would (will!) use. It has a clear progression with a nice balance of a great, big, fat toe up the rear! Dan comes across as caring and knowledgeable. His enthusiasm for his subject matter and a quality, finished product for your reader are also evident."

—Kelly K. Vriezen, president, Kelly Vriezen Leadership Group

"Dan gave me the confidence to move forward to write my book. His seminar gave me the blueprint to follow as well as practical tips to get it done."

—Pam Solberg-Tapper, executive coach

"A superb must-read book that quickly captures the critical book genres that are the why that should drive your writing, from legacy and manifesto to how-to and prove a point."

—Henry DeVries, author, *Marketing with a Book* and *Persuade with a Story*

"I wanted to say how much I enjoyed your book-writing webinar. I am a multipublished author but found some fresh ideas. Bravo!"

—Terry Schmidt, author, *Strategic Project Mastery*

"*Write Your Book in a Flash* contains dozens of great tips and ideas, but my favorite is Dan's section on research. If you follow his advice (which I intend to do when I begin work on my next nonfiction manuscript!), you'll have more than enough interesting, original material to fill your book."

—Jill N. Noble-Shearer, author and freelance editor

"Working with Dan has been like a master class in book writing. He is much more than a writing coach—he is a muse, teacher and friend, who makes the process enjoyable. This has been a great learning experience. I could not make this book happen without his expertise and support."

—Alan Cohen, executive coach, author, *The Connection Challenge: How Executives Create Power and Possibility in the Age of Distraction*

"Dan Janal streamlines the book writing process for people who have great ideas, experiences and stories, but need a true partner to bring all of those ideas into book form (without going crazy along the way). I feel so lucky to have Dan on my side, helping me to fulfill my goal of writing my first book!"

—Stephanie Blackburn Freeth, founder, Adaptive Alternatives LLC, author, *The Nonprofit Strategy Tango: I Lead, You Follow and Together We Create Your Next Strategic Plan*

SECTION I. OVERCOMING THE BLANK CANVAS SYNDROME

CHAPTER 1

PLANNING YOUR MASTERPIECE

*"I believe that everyone has the ability to write a book.
Most would-be authors simply don't know where to start."*

—Brian Tracy

Do you have a book inside you that is dying to get out?

Do you know what you want to write but can't get your ideas out of your head and onto paper?

Are you tearing your hair out, trying to write your book?

Or are you one of the many thousands of people who have *started* writing a book but can't get past chapter 1?

You are not alone, my friend.

Millions of people don't *finish* writing a book.

But it isn't your fault. Marketing guru Seth Godin described this affliction in his book, *The Dip: A Little Book That Teaches You When to Quit (and When to Stick).* People start grand plans with noble intentions. Then they hit a dip, and they don't finish. Does this sound like you?

You decide you want to play the guitar. You tell everyone you know. You take a few lessons. You progress. Eventually, you hit a plateau, where you see little to no improvement. You practice for hours and spend money on lessons, but you still can't play anything for your friends without dying of embarrassment. You give up.

People hit this wall in almost everything they do—from trying to lose weight, to creating impossibly long to-do lists, to saving money for retirement. The people who succeed find a way to persevere when things get tough (or when you hit a dip/plateau).

The same is true with writers. They tell everyone they are going to write a book. Everyone congratulates them. The writers write a few chapters until they hit a wall.

Then one of several things happens: They give up because, frankly, writing a book takes time, energy, and discipline. Or they break through "the dip" and cross over to the other side.

Perhaps they found a coach who inspired them. Maybe they found a writing partner who cowrote the book or ghostwrote it for them. Maybe they developed a new mind-set to help them overcome beliefs holding them back.

Listen to what one of my webinar clients wrote to me—mind you, she'd written two books:

I have gotten 60 percent of my first draft done. Have lost energy, feel discouraged. How can I create a plan that will help me finish? It feels like a daunting task; I need to cut it down to size. I know that sounds SIMPLE, but it is not EASY.

Has this happened to you?

Relax! You are not alone. I'll show you many solutions you can use to overcome procrastination and conquer your limiting beliefs so you can write and *finish* your book.

I'll also provide you with many tips, tools, and exercises to help you start—and finish—your book. Everything you need to write *your* book is in *this* book. I will be your book coach, providing you with exercises and a new mind-set to push you through the dip so you can finish your book and start making your dreams come true.

HERE'S MY BIG PROMISE TO YOU

You can write a book you are proud of and a book that helps you reach your business goals. I won't say it is *easy*, but it can be done with less stress and more focus than you can possibly imagine. I'll show you how to make writing your book as easy as child's play.

When you were a kid, did you have a paint-by-numbers kit? Many people in my book-writing seminars did. When I asked them what they liked about it, they said:

- I knew what to do.

- I didn't have to worry about what color to choose.

- I would have a nice picture when I finished.

- I had a structure.

- It was fun.

- I couldn't paint without it.

I'd add one other benefit to the paint-by-numbers kit: You will know when you are done!

Think of a book outline as a giant checklist. As you write each section, you cross off each item. When you're done, you're done!

Instead of filling in outlines of birds, flowers, houses, and people, as in a paint-by-number, I'll show you how to create outlines of your chapters filled with colorful stories, vibrant ideas, and vivid words.

Let's have *fun* with your book!

WHY YOU MUST WRITE YOUR BOOK

My mission is to help people start—and finish—their books, so they can build their brands, expand their networks, influence more people, and make more sales.

Few things are worse than having a great idea locked inside your head. You need to share your message with the world.

Why am I so passionate about books?

I believe books can make a big impact and help people build their businesses.

People just like you write books that have the power to change lives....

Your own life.

Your readers' lives.

Yes, these are big goals. I like to aim high. I have a feeling you do too.

You're probably wondering, *Can a person like me really make an impact with a book?*

Yes. You can. My clients have written books that have helped people improve their lives, their businesses, their professions, their families, and their health.

People have read my books and thanked me for changing their lives. I wrote the first book about marketing on the Internet back in 1993—the *Online Marketing Handbook*—when most people didn't know what the Internet was.

I saw the opportunity. I wrote a book that showed the world how to market their products and services online. Because of my background working with online services such as CompuServe and America Online (I was on the PR team that launched AOL), I knew the potential of selling online. In the early 1990s, people didn't think commerce could be conducted on the Internet. Today *every* business has an Internet strategy. Brick and mortar stores are dying, as people today prefer to buy things online.

That book gave me credibility, which helped me land speaking engagements and consulting assignments. I spoke all around the world. I taught businesspeople how to use the Internet in Beijing, Budapest, and Rio de Janeiro, as well as all across the United States, Canada, and Mexico. I taught the first Internet marketing class at Berkeley and an Internet branding class at Stanford.

That one book changed my life—and those of tens of thousands of people worldwide who read my book, attended my seminars, webinars, podcasts, and teleseminars, as well as TV and radio appearances.

As a member of the National Speakers Association for twenty years, I've seen what books can do to help build businesses of literally thousands of people just like you. Books help thought leaders, business executives, consultants, coaches, and speakers:

- Become famous
- Spread ideas to influence their industries and the world
- Raise fees
- Meet new prospects and clients
- Stand out from competitors and win new business

- Find more prestigious speaking assignments, where they can influence larger and more powerful audiences
- Sell books to make money
- Give back to the community

Have you seen colleagues or competitors write books that have changed their businesses and their lives? Have you thought, *I could have done that!* Or worse: *I should have done that!*

I'm here to tell you: If you have a book inside you, you must share it with the world so you can take others from the dark into the light. This book will show you how.

DAN'S STORY

You're probably wondering who I am and why you should listen to me.

I've written more than a dozen books, including eight books for Wiley, one of the largest and most respected New York-based publishing houses. I've also self-published several others. Publishers have translated my books into Spanish, Portuguese, Korean, Japanese, Chinese, German, and Hungarian.

Let's put that into perspective.

I wrote those eight books for Wiley in just over seven years. Yes, more than one book a year. Those weren't teensy, tiny, twenty-four-page e-books, with large type and wide margins. These books each had two hundred-plus pages of original insights and in-depth research.

If you think I've cracked the code for writing books, you're right: I have—and now I will share those ideas with you in this book.

That's because I realized my "superpower" is to bring order out of chaos. I know how to inspire people like you to gather your thoughts and create an outline that will help you write your book in a flash!

When I look at my career, my superpower makes perfect sense.

I was a journalism student at Northwestern University. At that time, the school operated on a trimester system. We had ten weeks in a semester—not sixteen like other schools, which meant we had less time to do more work. Each student took four classes, and each class had three major assignments or tests—that's twelve major assignments or tests in only ten weeks. That's a lot of work to get done in a short time. That experience taught me four valuable lessons:

1. How to manage my time
2. How to get organized
3. How to figure out what was important
4. How to meet a deadline

I must have figured out the puzzle, because I graduated with a B-plus average in a school full of geniuses.

Here's a secret no one knows about me—until now. My SAT scores were among the lowest in the school—95 percent of the students in my class scored better than I did! You see, I needed to figure out how to learn fast, or I'd fall behind.

Fortunately, what I lacked in SAT skills, I made up for with creativity and ingenuity!

From there, I became a reporter for a daily newspaper. I researched and wrote three stories every day, five days a week, for four years. I learned how to work fast, research fast, write fast, and get the facts straight. You can't be sloppy when you know thousands of people will read your work.

With that background, it was only a matter of time before I wrote a book. And when I finally did, my ability to write fast paid off.

I realized many business executives and thought leaders wanted to make the world a better place by writing books. I knew I could help them write books by helping them clarify their ideas and boost their confidence.

When I decided to be a book-writing coach and ghostwriter, I took courses and developed new skills for writing and coaching. Now, I coach business and thought leaders by encouraging them and holding them accountable. I also work as a developmental editor who helps authors shape their books.

Because working on books takes a lot of time, I knew I could help only a few people at a time. I wrote this book so I could help you.

This book contains my writing tips and secrets, as well as tips from dozens of authors I've interviewed. If you truly want to write a book, you are in the right place. This book will help you plan, write, and finish your book.

WHAT'S YOUR STORY?

I've shared a little of my background. Now it's time for you to think about *your* story. Why do you want to write a book? Do you want:

- to get a better job?
- to increase your negotiating power for your next raise?
- to be invited to serve on prestigious boards?
- to increase your influence?
- more prestige?
- help getting to the next Big Thing?
- to build your brand, so you can get more clients?
- to increase your fame, so you can charge more money?
- to share your wisdom with future generations?
- to reinvent yourself?

Books can make these things happen.

Mark Faust, author of *High Growth Levers,* urges his clients to write books.

"The selling power of your own book is through the roof. Nothing matches the selling power and credentialing of your own book," he said. "You don't make anything from the book, but you can make hundreds of thousands of dollars, or much more, from the business only your own book can help you to capture."

Val Wright, author of **Thoughtfully Ruthless: The Key to Exponential Growth***,* said,

"Before you start writing, you need to know why you want to write a book. As a leadership and innovation expert, my clients kept telling me that I had to write a book to share my ideas and stories with a broader audience. I wrote my book to help executives and entrepreneurs rapidly grow their business, magically create more time, and boost their energy."

YOUR TURN: WHY DO YOU WANT TO WRITE A BOOK?

Write the main reason why you want to write a book. If you aren't sure, don't worry. In the next chapter, you'll see how many people just like you decided to write a book.

THE TEN ESSENTIAL STEPS TO WRITING YOUR BOOK IN A FLASH

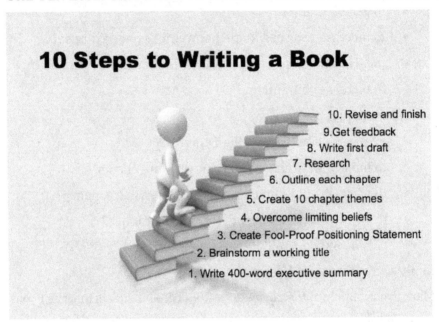

10 Steps to Writing a Book

10. Revise and finish
9. Get feedback
8. Write first draft
7. Research
6. Outline each chapter
5. Create 10 chapter themes
4. Overcome limiting beliefs
3. Create Fool-Proof Positioning Statement
2. Brainstorm a working title
1. Write 400-word executive summary

Figure 1: Writing a book is easier when you follow these steps. (Images provided by PresenterMedia.com)

Because I'm a marketing guy, as well as an author of more than ten books, I bring a unique perspective to writing a book. Rather than suggesting you do a "brain dump" as other book coaches suggest, I offer a structured system approach to writing your book. The overall themes are: How can I get my best prospects to buy this book? What do they need to see in the book to convince them to buy it? How can I deliver so much value they absolutely *must* have it?

To reach those goals, I've created this 10-step approach to put all those elements in place in an orderly way that helps you write the book you really want to write.

Here's an overview of the book-writing process. Start taking notes, and see how these steps fit into writing your book in a flash. We'll do several exercises to create your masterpiece quickly.

- Get focused. Write an executive summary, which is a short 400-word description of the book. Identify your ideal readers, and describe their main problem. Your book should provide an answer to that problem.

- Name it! Create a working title.

- Explain it to other people by creating a Fool-Proof Positioning Statement.

- Overcome limiting beliefs. We all have them. Let's tame them.

- Create ten chapter topics. These are your big ideas.

- Write a comprehensive outline for each chapter. Include lots of descriptions and examples to prove your points.

- Research the book.

- Write the first draft.

- Get feedback.

- Revise, edit, and finish.

This book shows you how to take these steps in specific detail. You'll pick up great pointers on how to write your book. I'll also refer you to other classic authorship books.

We'll work on assignments and exercises to help you with each task. I urge you to do these drills. If you do, you'll have created a wonderful outline that you can fill in as easily as a paint-by-numbers kit.

I'm sure you can do it! However, many people get stuck and never finish their books. Let's look at that sad phenomenon, so it doesn't happen to you.

WHY DON'T PEOPLE FINISH THEIR BOOKS?

Unfortunately, people don't finish their books for many reasons. Do any of these reasons sound like you?

- They aren't focused. They have so many ideas, they don't know what to keep or what to leave out or what order to put them in. I'll show you how to overcome this problem with exercises to keep you on track.

- They don't have enough information. Many people think they have all the information they need right inside their heads. Not so. Most people will run out of knowledge and ideas. I'll show you how to gather new information to make your book read better and make you look like the information impresario.

- They don't know when to stop. They either write and write and write, or they micromanage the editing process and sweat bullets over every word. Let's clarify those two issues: In the first case, you can bore people to death with too much information. In the second case, no one cares about your clever turn of the phrase. People want information. They know they aren't reading literature. If you solve their problems, you're a hero. If you don't help them, you're a zero.

- They do a "brain dump." What's wrong with a brain dump? You create a mess! You must have structure.

- They don't have "cheerleaders" to support them. Family members might not be supportive and enthusiastic. Get your family on board.

HOW TO GET THE MOST FROM THIS BOOK

You can learn a lot by reading this book, but you will get more value by completing the exercises. You'll find you really can write a book by painting by the numbers and filling in the blanks in these exercises. The book and the exercises are presented in a logical order. Read from beginning to end and do not skip chapters. In many cases, each exercise builds on a previous one. When you finish this book, you'll have your outline completed, and you'll be ready to write your book in a flash.

Download a printable version of this worksheet at
www.WriteYourBookInAFlash.com/worksheets

LET'S GET STARTED!

You have a desire to write a book. Now you'll have a plan. Here's what you'll discover on our journey through this adventure of writing a book.

SECTION 1: OVERCOMING THE BLANK CANVAS SYNDROME

Chapter 1—This chapter sets the tone for the book, introduces me (Dan Janal) as the author and coach who helps you through this process, gets you excited to continue, and shows you what to expect in the coming chapters.

Chapter 2—What *kind* of book do you want to write? We'll look at book formats and genres so you can pick the most suitable ones to help reach your goals.

Chapter 3—Get focused on the overall *mission* of your book by writing the executive summary.

Chapter 4—Let's give your book a *title* to capture the hearts and souls of your prospects.

Chapter 5—By now you'll have a clear idea of what the book is about, and you can create your elevator pitch, so you can explain the book to people. I've created "The Fool-Proof Positioning Statement" to help you easily craft this important message.

Chapter 6—Your frame of mind is a key factor. Will you write your book in a flash or will you join the thousands of wannabe authors who never finish their books? You'll find several easy ways to overcome limiting beliefs.

SECTION 2: MAPPING YOUR JOURNEY

Chapter 7—The secret sauce to writing a book fast is to create an empowering outline that is easy to follow. Forget what your high school teacher taught you about dry, boring outlines. The outlining technique I will teach you can be as fun as paint-by-number pictures—and just as pretty. You'll discover many inspiring reasons to write an outline.

Chapter 8—We dive into the nitty-gritty. You'll discover easy ways to outline chapters. We'll do a deep dive into those chapters themselves, so you'll know exactly where every point you to want make will have a home. You'll create the ten themes for the chapters. When you're done, you'll have your table of contents.

Chapter 9—Outline chapter 1. A great book starts with a great chapter.

Chapter 10—Outline chapters 2 through 9. The heart and soul of your book.

Chapter 11—Outline the final chapter. This is your call to action to engage readers to work with you or embrace your ideas.

Chapter 12—Create the book's front matter. You've done the heavy lifting. Now let's create material that goes at the beginning of your book.

Chapter 13—Create the book's back matter. We'll talk about what you need to write to close your book.

Chapter 14—Research. As you write the outline, you'll see holes in your story. In his chapter, you'll find places on the web to get the needed info. Plus, you'll discover ways to interview people who can provide original material for your book.

Chapter 15—Storytelling. People remember stories; they forget rules, theories, and ultimatums. You'll discover how easy it is to tell a memorable story with tips from a Hollywood story-writing legend who I interviewed.

SECTION 3: MAKE YOUR BOOK SHINE!

Chapter 16—The art of writing, editing, and revising. These writing tips will help you polish your text.

Chapter 17—Let's get feedback from peers and potential readers, so you know what works, what doesn't, and what's missing.

Chapter 18—Design tips to make your book unputdownable.

Chapter 19—Computers make it easy to write your book and your outline. We'll explore high-tech programs to help you—and remind you of a few low-tech methods. Your choice!

Section 4: Finishing Touches for Your Book: Putting it All Together and Next Steps

Chapter 20—Hire a book coach. Every professional athlete who makes millions of dollars has a coach. Shouldn't you have one too? You don't have to write your book alone. If you need help, you'll also learn how to find the right coach or ghostwriter.

Chapter 21—Next steps, plus final pointers to touch up your masterpiece.

Appendix

Resources—Links to important websites and books to help you.

What the Book Does Not Cover

This book contains a lot of great information. It doesn't cover:

- Grammar
- Traditional Publishing vs. Self-Publishing
- Marketing
- Distribution

Check Google for up-to-date articles on these topics, as book publishing changes rapidly.

Next Steps

Writing a book can be as easy and as fun as working with a paint-by-numbers kit. Many business executives and thought leaders have written books to spread their influence and reach their goals.

Now you have a good idea how this book will help you. Let's get started.

CHAPTER 2

WHAT KIND OF BOOK
DO YOU NEED TO WRITE?

Writing a book is easier than you think, especially if you tweet, blog, or speak. You might have enough content on your computer to write your book and not realize it. In this chapter, you'll see five different book formats. You can decide which format is best for you. Then we'll look at major book genres so you can model other successful books.

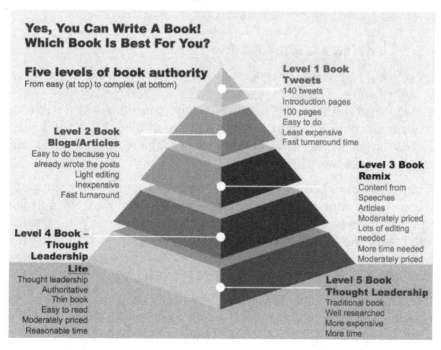

Figure 2: The Five Levels of Thought Leadership Books.
*(Images Provided by **PresenterMedia.com**)*

Yes, you *can* write a book!

The chart above shows five book formats, arranged from easiest to most difficult to produce. They also are arranged from credible to most credible. The key point is they are *all* credible! You can give any book to any prospect, and they'll think you are wonderful.

Use this guide to find the book style that will help you most:

- Tweets or Tips
- Blog Posts
- Remix or Curated Content
- Big Business Card
- Thought Leadership

Which book is the right one for you? It depends on your purpose. There's a style and a format that is right for everyone. Let's look at each book type, so you can decide which one meets your needs.

LEVEL 1 BOOK: TWEETS OR TIPS

If you have 140 tweets or tips, you can compile a thin book that shows your brilliance. This is the easiest book to produce because you've already written the material. It needs only to be edited. You will need to write overviews to introduce each group of thoughts. You can also include sales pages, so people can learn about your services and contact you for more information.

If you don't have 120 tweets or tips handy, you can create them easily if you review your speeches, podcasts, or interview transcripts. Or you can find a good interviewer who can ask you questions. Your answers will create the 120 tweets. **Think AHA** specializes in producing this book format. Putting this book together could take as little as eight hours, according to company president Mitchell Levy.

If you have powerful and insightful words and thoughts, this book can position you as a thought leader or as a trusted business partner—even though the book uses only a few words. Remember, readers today like short books and want to skim. If this sounds like your ideal reader, use this format.

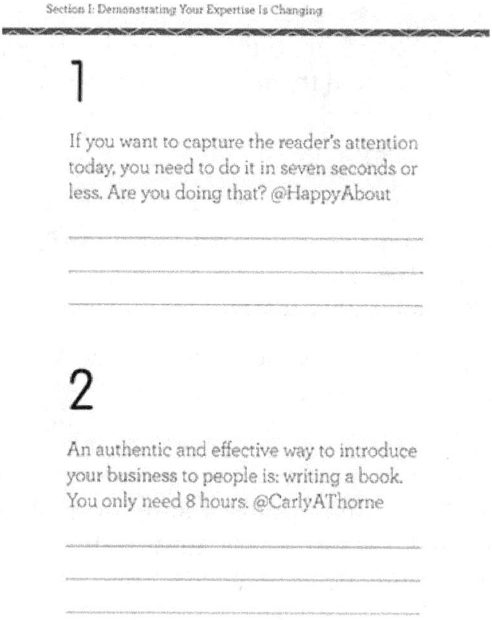

Section I: Demonstrating Your Expertise Is Changing

1

If you want to capture the reader's attention today, you need to do it in seven seconds or less. Are you doing that? @HappyAbout

_____

_____

_____

2

An authentic and effective way to introduce your business to people is: writing a book. You only need 8 hours. @CarlyAThorne

_____

_____

_____

Figure 3: AHA book sample page

Level 2 Book: Blog Posts

Thoughtful blogs transformed into a book will position you as a thought leader. People who like page-turning fiction and other short-form writing like this writing style.

A book composed of blog posts is almost as easy to produce as a tweets or tips book because once again, you have already created the content. It's longer, but it could be finished in just a few days.

You will need to create text and edit material for style and to fit on pages. You might decide to divide a long post into shorter ones, so they are easier to read. For example, instead of creating one long chapter on "Ten Ways to Write a Book," you might create two chapters—one called "Five Ways to Write a Book" and another called "Five More Ways to Write a Book."

One of my clients, Lisa M. Anderson, created a book from her blog posts, *I've Been Thinking: Turning Everyday Interactions into Profitable Opportunities*. She told me it was a relatively easy process. She rewrote some posts to provide even more information. Her posts varied in length. She wanted them all to be nearly the same size for the book, so she added information to some and trimmed others. Then she hired a copy editor to polish her work.

Another client who used blogs for her book, Kris Putnam-Walkerly, won several awards for her book, *Confident Giving: Sage Advice for Funders*. The awards prove that blog-based books can carry credibility and accolades for authors.

Although Richard Carlson did not write blogs when he created the best-selling book *Don't Sweat the Small Stuff*, it might be the perfect book for you to model. Each chapter is blog size, about 600 words.

If you are a prolific blogger, you may have enough content to create multiple books. Rather than publish all your content directly from your blog, you might want to talk to an editor or book coach to determine which topics your readers or prospects want to read in book format. An outside perspective might help you get focused and provide more value.

LEVEL 3 BOOK: REMIX-CURATED CONTENT SPEECHES/TRANSCRIPTS BOOK

This book is based on material you created. As a thought leader or business executive, you have probably created a lot of material in the form of speeches, presentations, reports, interviews, and podcasts. Select the best ideas from your existing material, as well as adding new information or writing new overviews for sections.

This book could take a few weeks to create. As with the blog post book, this book type contains short thoughtful pieces, so you will be seen as a thought leader. It also appeals to people who like to read in bite-sized chunks.

Case Study: Turn Training Materials into Books. *Reporters Are Looking for YOU!*

I wrote *Reporters Are Looking for YOU!* from a set of ninety tips I created to teach new clients who bought my publicity service, PR LEADS. If you have a training series, you can convert it into a book. Here's how I did it.

When a new client signs up for PR LEADS, chances are they don't know a thing about publicity or how to work with a reporter. I wanted to teach my clients these tips and tricks to help them get ahead. But there's a lot to learn, and while it isn't difficult, most people can't absorb a lot of material in one sitting. I created a series of ninety tips. My computer would automatically send one tip a day to each client.

Many clients told me they loved those tips. I knew I had great content to share, so I turned those tips into a book. As you might imagine, it was pretty easy to accomplish, since I had already created the information. I changed the formatting and double-checked the spelling. To make the book more logical and easy to read, I rearranged the tips by topics such as "Writing," "Editing," "Interview Skills," and "Marketing."

I spent a week creating the book. I hired an editor and cover designer to bring the book up to par. After they finished in just a few days, I self-published the book on Amazon.

If you have created content that can be reused, you can quickly and easily create a book that builds your credibility and helps your readers.

Level 4 Book: Thought Leadership Lite or Big Business Card

A Thought Leadership Lite book, also known as a Big Business Card book, builds credibility so you can stand out from the crowd, get new business, and charge higher fees. For executives, these books can open doors to more challenging and rewarding careers.

These books have about 20,000 words (about 150 pages). While these books look thin, you can say a lot in 150 pages. Readers love short books because they can read them on an airplane or in a few reading sessions.

Many professionals choose this type of book because they are easy to write and relatively short, yet they're still long enough to be credible. Depending on the material you have already created (or need to create), you could write this book in a few days or weeks.

These books will help you generate ideas:

Push: A Guide to Living an All Out Life: The Story of Orange Fitness, by Ellen Latham, founder of Orange Theory Fitness. The book told her story: how she got started in the fitness industry, how she decided to go out on her own, how she developed a unique concept, and more. The words "push" and "all out" are part of her specialized, branded vocabulary. This wordplay reinforces her brand.

Dean Minuto published part of his seminar in a book called ***The One-Page Sales Coach.*** The book contains his spoken content, visual elements, and assignments. Anyone who attended his seminar would consider it a good refresher. It serves as a big business card that shows prospects what he can deliver in a seminar.

I've seen a variety of big business card books; however, they can go in many different directions. For example:

- Ten business principles in ten chapters
- A reworked transcript of a three-hour training seminar
- A long sales letter that has good tips and facts
- The company founder's history and mission

LEVEL 5 BOOK: THOUGHT LEADERSHIP

These are the 160–250 page hardcover books you expect to see in a bookstore.

To create this book, you can use your previously written materials, in-depth research, and commentary. Obviously, these books take more time to plan and write.

This traditional book is the most complex to produce. It could take as little as three or four months, but six or seven months is more likely.

As you might imagine, this is the most credible book—not to take anything away from the other books. However, this thought leadership book sets the gold standard. Readers see it as a "real" book that sits alongside true bestsellers, like *Good to Great* and *7 Habits of Highly Effective People*, with thoughtful pieces and lots of case studies to prove their paradigm-shattering hypotheses.

WHAT SHOULD BE INCLUDED IN A THOUGHT LEADERSHIP BOOK?

Your thought leadership book must answer these questions:

- What do people **need** to know?
- What do people **want** to know?
- What do you need to **show** them to build your brand or to get the business?

Remember, you are not writing the encyclopedia of this topic. Your book must convince readers to take action or to position themselves properly to reach their objectives. Anything that supports those goals, you keep. Anything that detracts from those goals, you cut. When you've proven your points, you're done.

DOES SIZE MATTER?

Nonfiction books can have any number of pages. E-books can be a few pages long or as long as a traditional book. Nonfiction books tend to be about 50,000 words. How-to books and self-help books run about 40,000 to 50,000 words. Business books can be even shorter—for instance, *Who Moved My Cheese?* has only 96 pages and fewer than 30,000 words.

Remember, no one cares how many words your book contains. They care about reading the right content.

However, I do have one rule that you can't break: a printed book should contain at least 100–125 pages, so your name and title will fit on the spine.

CASE STUDY: DOES BOOK SIZE MATTER?

Back in 1994, I spoke at a conference for the National Speakers Association. After my talk, a woman came up to me and started a conversation. It went something like this:

Woman: I loved your talk.

Me: Thank you very much.

Woman: I see you wrote a book. It looks very authoritative.

Me: Thank you very much.

Woman: I have one question.

Me: Ask me anything! I'm here to help!

Woman: Do I have to read all of it?

That conversation took place more than twenty years ago. People's attention spans have only become shorter in the intervening years!

Another author at the conference wrote a thin book on how to market on the Internet in a weekend. He sold a lot more books than I did!

Lesson learned. Don't fear short books.

YOUR TURN: SELECT YOUR BOOK STYLE

Which book type will help you most? Make your selection based on your budget, your time frame, the amount of material you have already written—or will need to write—and your reader's attention span.

Write the answer here:

_____

MAJOR BOOK GENRES

The founder of Papa John's pizza franchise, John H. Schnatter, wrote **Papa: The Story of Papa John's Pizza**. He told *BusinessWeek* he wrote the book, "for my kids, grandkids, and franchisees, so they would know how we did this." He wrote the book to leave a legacy.

Other business executives write books to prove a point, be significant, teach, inspire, be a thought leader, or leave a mark on the world.

What's your motivation to write a book?

After working with thousands of speakers, authors, coaches, thought leaders, and small-business professionals who have written books, I've seen these major genres. You might model these examples:

- **Legacy.** Business executives who want to leave their mark on the world and to help future generations will write memoirs. These books include tips for success and stories of overcoming obstacles. Suggested reading: ***Basic Black: The Essential Guide for Getting Ahead at Work (and in Life)*** by Cathie Black, first female publisher of *USA TODAY*. ***Uncontainable: How Passion, Commitment, and Conscious Capitalism Built a Business Where Everyone Thrives*** by Kip Tindell, founder of the Container Store.

- **Tools.** Similar to legacy books, executives write these books to share ideas that brought them their successes. Their motivations could be personal branding and helping others. Examples include ***The Real Life MBA*** by Jack Welch and Suzy Welch or ***The 4-Hour Workweek*** by Tim Ferriss.

- **Manifesto.** Authors who are visionaries, have a certain point of view, or want to change the world write these books. They want their readers to take up their causes. I've read manifestos on new ways of thinking about using the Internet, customer service, and many other topics. Suggested reading: ***Good to Great*** by Jim Collins. ***Thinking, Fast and Slow*** by Daniel Kahneman. Any book by Seth Godin. ***Setting the Table: The Transforming Power of Hospitality in Business*** by Danny Meyer, founder of Shake Shack. ***Conscious Capitalism: Liberating the Heroic Spirit of Business*** by John Mackey, copresident of Whole Foods.

- **Proof.** Authors present a hypothesis. They use case studies and statistics to prove their points. These authors—usually consultants at well-respected companies—want to establish their thought leadership. Suggested reading: ***The Tipping Point*** by Malcolm Gladwell. ***Freakonomics*** by Steven Levitt and Stephen Dubner.

- **How-To**. Perhaps the most popular kind of book shows readers how to do something. Suggested reading: ***How to Win Friends and Influence People*** by Dale Carnegie. ***Life Is Good: How to Live with Purpose and Enjoy the Ride*** by Bert Jacobs and John Jacobs, founders of Life Is Good.

- **Process.** These books offer research and show how to perform a task. Suggested reading: ***Influence*** by Robert Cialdini, PhD. ***The Only Negotiating Guide You'll Ever Need*** by Peter B. Stark and Jane Flaherty.

- **Training.** These books are extensions of educational sessions. Suggested reading: ***Loyal for Life*** by John Tschohl.

- **Fictional.** These books use fictional stories to show why certain business principles work. Suggested reading: ***The Go Giver*** by Bob Burg and John David Mann. ***Who Moved My Cheese?*** by Ken Blanchard and Spencer Johnson, MD.

- **Inspirational.** Books offering motivational tips. Suggested reading: ***Lifestorming*** by Alan Weiss and Marshall Goldsmith.

YOUR TURN: CHOOSE YOUR BOOK GENRE

Which genre sounds like the book you want to write? Which book will help you build your business? Write your answer here.

Can you think of a book that was so well done, you wish you'd written it—with the same tone and authority—but with *your* content? Write the title here or on a piece of paper.

Now you should have a book to model.

NEXT STEPS

Now that you have a good idea of the book you want to write, let's focus on the overall message of your book.

CHAPTER 3

THE BIG PICTURE

Details create the big picture.

—Sandford I. Weill

Imagine you are searching for a book on Amazon. After seeing the title and the book cover, you read the book's short description. Does it give you a great reason to read the book? Do you say to yourself, "The author understands me and my problem! I have to buy this book!"

Your readers will buy your book if you write a great book summary. Best-selling authors start writing their books with the book description. This exercise helps you get focused and lets your ideal readers know immediately if they want to buy your book.

If you write the executive summary first, you'll have an easier time writing the outline and the book. Plus, when someone asks what your book is about, you'll answer clearly and confidently.

The first step toward getting focused on writing your nonfiction business book is to write an executive summary—your book's essence. It answers these questions:

- What is the book about?
- Who is the ideal reader?
- What problem do you solve for them?
- How will they benefit from reading the book?
- Why is your book better than competing books?
- Why are you the right person to write the book?

This assignment will keep you focused, and once you're finished with your executive summary, you will have created the first piece of marketing material to promote your book. You will use this summary as the basis for the sales material printed on the back cover and on Amazon.

YOUR TURN: WRITE THE EXECUTIVE SUMMARY

Answer the preceding questions in 400 words in this space:

Download a printable version of this worksheet at
www.WriteYourBookInAFlash.com/worksheets

After you write the answers, turn them into a narrative or a story, as I did in the example. Here is the executive summary for this book—402 words.

EXECUTIVE SUMMARY FOR WRITE YOUR BOOK IN A FLASH

Do you want to know the secret to writing a nonfiction business book without wasting time or money?

Write Your Book in a Flash shows business executives, entrepreneurs, and thought leaders how to get focused fast, so they can write their book without tearing their hair out.

Most people dream of writing a book, but they never do. They either have too many ideas or not enough. Simply put, they aren't organized.

The secret to completing a book quickly is to have a system. Unlike books that show you *why* you should write a book, this book actually shows you *how* to write a book! You'll discover:

- How to write an outline and have fun doing it

- How to get stunning testimonials to help sell your book

- How to find and manage beta readers who will share honest feedback before the book is published

- How to research interesting ideas, stories, and facts so you never run out of ideas or information

- How to overcome "The Imposter Syndrome" and other limiting beliefs that stifle nearly every would-be author

- Clear examples that show you what to do

- Empowering exercises that show you how to write better and faster

- Simple how-to steps anyone can follow

- A paint-by-numbers system for writing a book!

Even if you hate to write, you'll finally feel good about writing your book. Most importantly, you'll get the job done!

This is the perfect book to read if you are a thought leader, entrepreneur, or business executive who wants to write a business book to build your personal brand, open doors to new opportunities, and leave a legacy of wisdom to future generations. Business leaders who write books get more clients at higher fees, have more impact, develop more credibility, and have more visibility where it matters most: in front of clients, customers, and prospects.

Unlike other books on writing, *Write Your Book in a Flash* doesn't debate the pros and cons of self-publishing vs. traditional publishing. Instead, it shows how to use your own work style and personal strengths, preferences, and personality so you can write the book you were meant to share with the world.

Dan Janal has written more than a dozen books that help businesses build their brands, including seven books for publishing giant Wiley. He is an award-winning daily newspaper reporter and business newspaper editor. As a publicity and marketing expert, he has helped more than 10,000 authors and experts build their platforms over the past 16 years. He holds bachelor's and master's degrees in journalism from Northwestern University's famed Medill School of Journalism.

AVOID MISTAKES WITH BOOK POSITIONING

Don't say the book is for everyone. Here's why:

- Very few books are for everyone.

- You can't afford to market the book to everyone.

- No one wants to buy a book for everyone. They want to buy a book that speaks to them. Think of women's health or men's health; those two markets have different concerns.

SHORTENING YOUR EXECUTIVE SUMMARY

When you look at the back of other books, you'll see the sales copy is much shorter than 400 words. So why do you need to write 400 words?

For starters, you can write 400 words more easily than 50 words. When you write 50 words, you limit yourself. You edit as you write. You cut words and ideas. You censor instead of create.

As you write, you will think of ideas, concepts, phrases, and words you would not have thought of if you had stopped at 50 words. You will get into a flow state that makes it easier to express yourself.

YOUR TURN: TRIM YOUR 400-WORD DESCRIPTION TO 50 WORDS

Mark Twain famously said, "I didn't have time to write you a short letter, so I wrote a long one instead."

The same is true with your executive summary book description. Now that you have written 400 words, chop it to 50!

I know that sounds cruel because you love each word! However, Amazon and the back cover can fit only so many words. Would you rather cut those words, or would you rather have someone else cut them for you? Either way, words *will* be cut because readers lose interest quickly.

Here's my 50-word version:

Write Your Book in a Flash shows business executives, entrepreneurs, and thought leaders how to write their book without tearing their hair out. Learn the paint-by-numbers system so you can have fun sharing your ideas. Thought-provoking exercises guide you to success.

Write your 50-word description here:

_____

_____

_____

_____

_____

_____

YOUR TURN: RESEARCH COMPETING BOOKS

If you'd like more help writing your summary, why not review your competitors? Use Amazon to find five books that compete with yours and rank high on Amazon's sales charts. Read their descriptions. What do you like about them? What don't you like about them? You'll see how your competitors have succeeded and you might see features you can improve.

Book 1:_____

Name_____

What do you like about the description?

Book 2:_____

Name_____

What do you like about the description?

Book 3:_____

Name_____

What do you like about the description?

Book 4:_____

Name_____

What do you like about the description?

Book 5:_____

Name_____

Download a printable version of this worksheet at
www.WriteYourBookInAFlash.com/worksheets

NEXT STEPS

Executives demand to see an executive summary for any long report. Why should your readers expect anything less from you? The executive summary gets you focused—and it helps market the book.

In the next chapter, we'll refine that message further, so you can easily share your book's vision with everyone you meet. You'll find out how to get focused fast.

CHAPTER 4

FRAMING YOUR MESSAGE

A brand becomes stronger when you narrow its focus.

—Al Ries

Hardly a day goes by without a new author calling me on the phone, asking me if I will help promote his or her book. I ask one simple question:

What is your book about?

You'd think they'd answer that question easily, but you'd be wrong.

Surprisingly, in most cases, for the next twenty minutes, authors tell me everything *but* what the book is about! They talk about how long they worked on the book, how many pages it has, how they tried to find a publisher, and how a printer ripped them off. But they cannot tell me what the book is about!

You need to be able to tell anyone about the book in a few seconds so they understand immediately. In my seminars, I teach a formula I created and call "The Fool-Proof Positioning Statement." I've taught this formula for nearly 30 years in several countries and in several languages. It always works!

In this chapter, I'll share my formula for getting focused fast, so you can tell anyone—even your grandmother—about your book in two sentences.

Two simple sentences comprise this formula. Here's the first:

MY BOOK TITLE is a CATEGORY that helps PRIMARY AUDIENCE achieve PRIMARY BENEFIT.

For example:

Write Your Book in a Flash is a writing-skills book that helps business executives write books quickly.

You've probably seen variations of this exercise called an "elevator pitch" or a "positioning statement." If you have a format you like better, feel free to experiment.

STEP 1: DEFINE YOUR CATEGORY

One great feature of the Fool-Proof Positioning Statement is that you tell people the exact category into which your book fits, so they can immediately see if they want to read it.

People have a basic need to put things into categories. If you don't tell them what category your book belongs in, they will try to find a category on their own, so they can make sense of it. And let me tell you, people are horrible mind readers! They will not think of what you expect them to think. In fact, you *must* tell them your book is a *book*.

For example, if I said, "*Write Your Book in a Flash* will help thought leaders become more influential," people would have no idea if this was a book, a seminar, a DVD, a coaching program, or a new pop single. Instead, when I tell them that *Write Your Book in a Flash* is a *book* that will help thought leaders become more influential, they know I am talking about a book, not a seminar, or a course, or a lecture.

Your category could be business, careers, stress management, negotiating, fitness, leadership, or customer service.

For example, you could say:

- *Write Your Nonprofit's Strategic Plan Now* is a guide and workbook that helps nonprofit boards create their strategic plan with an easy-to-follow, step-by-step process.

- *I've Been Thinking About* is a business innovation book that helps small business owners find creative solutions.

- *The Connection Challenge* is a leadership book that helps executives create an engaged workforce.

STEP 2: DEFINE YOUR PRIMARY AUDIENCE

You want to focus on one key market. In fact, marketers want you to focus on *one key buyer*. They call this person an "avatar," a detailed description of your ideal client. That includes demographics, psychographics, fears, and motivations.

Although this exercise is fairly well known among marketers, I first learned it at a seminar hosted by Christian Mickelsen, a coach who teaches coaches. Let me paraphrase what he told us:

> "My ideal client is named Judy. She's 44 years old and has two kids. She drives an older model SUV and has spent two thousand dollars on coaching seminars online. She wants to be a coach, but she has trouble asking for the order. When she gets a client, she doesn't charge enough. She wants to help make the world a better place, so she works with people who say they have no money. Her husband says, 'When are you going to make money with this coaching thing?'"

Suddenly, forty middle-aged women burst out laughing. They might not all have been named "Judy," but otherwise they fit the description!

That's pretty specific, wouldn't you agree? As I looked around the room and noted that another person and I were the only men, it became apparent Christian knew his market.

Ideal Client Worksheet

While many people could benefit from your book, who is your ideal client? Use this worksheet to describe your ideal client:

- Name
- Age
- Gender
- Family situation (if appropriate)
- Income
- Education level
- Job title
- Industry sector
- Biggest problem or fear
- Goals
- Values
- What do they read?

- What do they watch?
- Who do they respect?
- What do they do for fun?

Add as much personal or professional data as you want.

STEP 3: FOCUS ON ONE PRIMARY BENEFIT

Readers buy your book to solve a problem. When you show them why or how they can benefit, they are more likely to buy your book. You can probably think of many reasons people should buy your book. Unfortunately, the brain can hold only a few bits of information before it becomes confused or tunes out. Therefore you need to think of the *one* key benefit that will turn people on.

For example, people might buy this book to:

- Overcome writer's block
- Spread their influence
- Become famous
- Take their business to the next level
- Stand out from the competition

On the back cover, list one killer benefit. When you talk to people one-on-one, you might use a different benefit that speaks to them. You can adapt the message to every prospect. But when you write the back cover, focus.

Use this worksheet to list five benefits or problems that will help your prospective readers overcome:

1._____

2._____

3._____

4._____

5._____

Now circle the best one for your back cover.

Step 4: Write Your Fool-Proof Positioning Statement, First Sentence

Now it is your turn to create your Fool-Proof Positioning Statement! Simply fill in the blank spots on this template.

[Title] is a [category] that helps [primary audience] achieve [primary benefit].

Note: Don't overthink this.

Pretend you are talking to your grandmother, who knows nothing about what you do. What would you say to her when she asks you what your book is about?

Step 5: Second Sentence Fool-Proof Positioning Statement

The real brilliance of the Fool-Proof Positioning Statement is that it contains *two* sentences, not one. As good as that first sentence is, your listener thinks, "Okay, I know five other books that do the same thing. Why should I buy *your* book?" That's why I created a second sentence to answer that question.

Unlike other [category] books, [book title] has/contains/helps people [primary differentiating point].

For example, the second sentence for this book could be:

- Unlike other writing-skills books, *Write Your Book in a Flash* has exercises that turn ideas into action.

- Unlike other writing-skills books, *Write Your Book in a Flash* was written by an author who has written many books.

- Unlike other writing-skills books, *Write Your Book in a Flash* focuses on creating a highly detailed outline to help you write faster.

- Unlike other writing-skills books, *Write Your Book in a Flash* doesn't bore you to death with lessons about grammar, punctuation, and style.

Yes, it is simple. Most would-be authors complicate the process. They add too many audiences, and they add too many benefits.

People get overwhelmed when they hear or see multiple pieces of information! You must make your book easy to understand.

Now let's do the second sentence. What makes your book different?

Unlike other [book category], [title] has [key differentiating feature].

List five differentiating features.

1._____

2._____

3._____

4._____

5._____

Circle the one you like the best.

STEP 6: PUTTING IT ALL TOGETHER

Use this space to write both sentences in your Fool-Proof Positioning Statement:

Download a printable version of this worksheet at **www.WriteYourBookInAFlash.com/worksheets**

NEXT STEPS

Many authors can't describe their books quickly or accurately. The Fool-Proof Positioning Statement helps you tell your target readers why they should get excited and want to read your book. You can always customize the statement to meet the needs of each person you meet and each audience you speak to.

Since you are birthing a book, let's name it.

CHAPTER 5

GIVE YOUR BOOK A COLORFUL TITLE!

A great title should jump off the page and grab people's attention.

—Henry DeVries

People *do* judge books by their covers. And they will decide to buy your book based, in part, on its title. You need to create a title that resonates with your audience.

You'll learn several techniques to create great titles for your book and chapters. But first I ask you to answer these questions to unleash your creativity. The answers will help you create your title with tactics shown later in this chapter.

YOUR TURN: WRITE THE ANSWERS TO THESE QUESTIONS.

1. What is your book's big promise?

2. What problem does your book solve?

Download a printable version of this worksheet at **www.WriteYourBookInAFlash.com/worksheets**

START WITH A WORKING TITLE

If you create a great title on your first try, you'd be like a golfer who hits a hole in one. It happens, but rarely. Don't waste time trying to create the perfect title when you begin to write. Don't stop writing because you are stuck thinking of a title either. Simply write a title. It's okay if you don't love it; you can change it later.

YOUR TURN:

Write the title here. The working title of my book is:

_____

DON'T GET MARRIED TO YOUR WORKING TITLE

During the writing process, you may discover a better title. Look what happened to one of my clients who edited a book.

"The working title was *Forget Everything You Know about Hiring.* During the writing, the title morphed into *You're Not the Person I Hired* (a comment made by someone we interviewed)," says Henry DeVries, CEO of Indie Books International.

You can—and probably will—change the title over time as the book develops. The original title of this book was *How to Create an Outline for Your Book.* Ugh! That title told what the book was about, but it wasn't catchy. It also didn't convey a benefit to readers. Why would they want to write an outline for their book?

I changed the title to *Write Your Book in a Flash.* It appeals to more people, has an impactful, action-oriented message, and conveys a benefit.

In marketing, we call this the benefit of the benefit. Here's a classic example: People don't buy drills to make holes; they buy drills to build houses or to hang curtains. Do you see the difference?

WHAT MAKES A GREAT TITLE?

A great title stands by itself. It needs no further description. Look at these perennial bestsellers:

- *How to Win Friends and Influence People*
- *Think and Grow Rich*
- *The One-Minute Manager*

Some titles hint at benefits:

- *Good to Great*

- *Made to Stick*

- *StrengthsFinder 2.0*

- *The Five Dysfunctions of a Team*

- *The 4-Hour Workweek*

A third group of titles have become bestsellers because they are cute or had a great marketing campaign behind them. That's hard to duplicate, so we won't discuss that.

Gimmicky titles confuse readers. Confused readers don't buy books.

"Don't be so cutesy or vague people don't get it," says Lois Creamer, marketing coach.

Let's focus on what makes the first group of titles work. What do they have in common? Simple: they tell people what they will get.

- You will win friends and influence people.

- You will think and grow rich.

- You will manage your team quickly.

Consumers have to make only one decision: Do I want this benefit? If the answer is yes, she buys the book. If the answer is no, she doesn't.

No one can own or copyright a book title, so don't worry if you come up with the perfect book title only to find that another book has the same or a similar title.

If you want to create an empire around your book or your topic, think of a way to brand the work with a title that can be adapted to different audiences and markets. For example:

- The 7 Habits of Highly Effective People (A later version focused on teens.)

- *Chicken Soup for the Soul* (Dozens of editions followed for such groups as women, prisoners, pet lovers, and golfers.)

CREATE BOOK AND CHAPTER TITLES—SAM HORN METHOD

You must create cool-sounding titles for your book and chapter headings. After all, chapter 2 and chapter 5 are not compelling titles.

Sam Horn, author of **POP**: *Create the Perfect Pitch, Title, and Tag Line for Anything,* has a terrific formula for creating book titles and chapter titles. She likes to link your topic and your hobby. It's a clever idea, and it could work for you.

Here's an example: Let's say you are a financial planner and an avid golfer. Think of the sayings about golf. For example, going for the green, take a mulligan, driving for the distance, the eighteenth green, hole in one. Each phrase could turn into a title relating to financial planning. For example, "Going for the Green: How to Turn Your Savings into a Gold Mine." That sounds better than "How to Turn Your Savings into a Gold Mine." This technique gives your book a personality.

I used this exercise in this book. My original chapter titles stunk. I created the paint-by-numbers idea and realized I love art. I brainstormed art terms, went online, and searched for other art terms. I wrote them down. Then I let my creativity flow. The chapter titles you see came from that exercise. Some are great. Some are good. I cut ones that stunk. *Release Your Inner Rembrandt?* Nope. If your titles are too cute, you may please yourself with your wit, but you could turn off readers.

My coaching client Stephanie Freeth used this technique to create this wonderful title based on her love of dancing: *The Nonprofit Strategy Tango: I lead, you follow and together we create your nonprofit's next strategic plan.* Her chapter headings included:

- "Are you ready to dance? Getting ready for strategic planning"
- "Envisioning your next production" (mission, values and financial sustainability)
- "Choreographing your steps" (goals, objectives, strategies)
- "The technical rehearsal" (reaching initial consensus)
- "The dress rehearsal" (allocating resources, measuring success, approving the plan)
- "Post planning: your show is in production with a 3–5 year run (implementation and accountability)."

If she can do this for a business topic, can't you?

YOUR TURN: CONVERT YOUR HOBBIES INTO TITLES

Answer these questions:

- What hobbies do you have?

- What phrases or terms are commonly understood?

- Turn the terms into book and chapter titles. (You might need to do this after you've outlined the chapters in your book. Come back to this exercise after you finish writing your table of contents.)

Use your intuition and creativity to make unique titles. You might have a lot of fun working on this!

LET GOOGLE HELP YOU CREATE YOUR TITLES

Here's another brainstorming technique. Go to Google and type a word into the search bar and add one letter at the end of the word. Google will guess what you are trying to type and will show you its results. This is its autofill function. For example, if you were writing a book about innovation and creativity, you might go to Google and type the word "brain" and a letter. For example, brain a, brain b, brain c, and so on. Google shows:

Brain

Brain dump

Brain dead

Brain jolt

Brain jack

Brain killer

Brainology

Brain pop

Brain power

Brainstorm

Brain teasers

Brainwash

Brain freeze

Brain fart

Brain food

Wouldn't you agree these words or phrases could be good chapter titles or subheads for a book about creativity?

YOUR TURN: USE GOOGLE TO FIND TITLE IDEAS

Go to Google and type your top three keywords with the additional letter. Write your best answers here:

Download a printable version of this worksheet at **www.WriteYourBookInAFlash.com/worksheets**

TESTING YOUR TITLE

In the early stages of writing, you won't be overly concerned with titles. As you get closer to finishing, however, you will want to get feedback on your title. Who do you think is the worst person to ask for feedback? No, it is not your mother. The worst person to ask is *you,* because you are *not* the target buyer of your book. You don't think like them. You don't buy like them. To find out what your prospects think of your title, you must ask them. If you belong to a professional organization that includes your target buyers, ask them.

GET FEEDBACK FROM YOUR FACEBOOK FRIENDS OR BLOG E-ZINE READERS

You can ask your blog e-zine readers or friends on Facebook to select their favorite title. Here's a sample post you can use. It shows possible subtitles for this book.

I'm coming out with a new book, and I'd like your help with selecting the perfect title. Which of the following titles would compel you to buy the book? Please tell me if you like a, b, c, d, or e:

A. A Paint-by-Numbers System to Write a Book to Take Your Business to the Next Level—FAST!

B. A Paint-by-Numbers System to Write a Book That Leaves Your Legacy—FAST!

C. A Paint-by-Numbers System to Write a Book That Grows Your Business—FAST!

D. Paint-by-Numbers System to Write a Book to Share Your Ideas—FAST!

E. Paint-by-Numbers System to Write a Book that Brands You as an Expert—FAST!

Download a printable version of this worksheet at
www.WriteYourBookInAFlash.com/worksheets

This looks pretty simple, eh?

Actually, there's a lot going on here you might not realize.

Let me point out the key tactic. Use the letter system (a, b, c, d, or e). That way, people simply type a letter. If you didn't have the letter, they'd have to type the title. They might not do that, because typing takes more time. Also, they might inadvertently type it incorrectly. That can happen easily if you have several titles that have the same words but in a different order as my sample shows.

Also, notice the phrase, "Which of the following titles would compel you to *buy* the book." That is a lot different from asking, "Which title do you *like* best?"

This seemingly simple message has hidden elements you might not appreciate at first glance. Carefully follow this model to get the info to select the best title.

YOUR BOOK TITLE BECOMES YOUR BRAND

Once you have a great title, make sure you own all the intellectual property around it.

Before you announce your title to the world, make sure the title is available as a website and on Facebook. If someone else has bought that name, you might want to find a different title. If you use the same name, there could be confusion.

"Your title should also be the trifecta: book title, speech title, and dot-com URL, all the same," said Henry DeVries of Indie Book Publishing.

To check for a title, go to **www.whois.com** and type the name in the search tool. You'll see if the name is available. This tool also shows the availability of alternative domains such as .info and .net. You might decide to use those domains.

To check Facebook, simply go to Facebook and search for your title.

You could adopt a tactic from Hollywood, which adds "movie" to the title (i.e. "FlashtheMovie.com"). You could add the word "book" to the title (i.e. "FlashtheBook.com"). This might not be the most elegant solution, but if you love your title, this tactic might help.

NEXT STEPS

Cool. You have a tentative title for your book. When people ask you, "What's new?" You can say, "I'm writing a great new book. It's called [title]." It sounds real to you and to them.

Let's switch gears. In the next chapter, let's make sure your brain is revved up and ready to go! Let's overcome limiting beliefs.

CHAPTER 6

YOUR WRITE FRAME OF MIND

The art of writing is the art of discovering what you believe.
—Gustave Flaubert

Writing should flow from your mind onto the computer screen as easily as words flow from your mouth. If you are in a flow state when you write, you should have no trouble completing your book. I'm here to help you find your flow and remove obstacles that impede flow. *Flow* is the mental state of being completely immersed in an activity. You are so absorbed in this activity that you don't notice time passing.

If you find writing difficult—or hard at times and easier at others—you're not alone. Many writers, including successful professional writers, must overcome limiting beliefs holding them back from reaching their potential.

This chapter is devoted to getting you into the right frame of mind.

Let's face it: It is easy to write, but it is also easy to *not* write. It is easy to get distracted or discouraged.

Everyone has a voice inside his or her head saying, "You can't do this," or "Let's do this later."

In this chapter, I'll share limiting beliefs my seminar and webinar participants have told me they've experienced. I'll share ideas to overcome limiting beliefs. Then we'll look at several exercises to help you overcome *your* limiting beliefs.

You might wonder why I'm asking you to overcome limiting beliefs. The previous chapters helped you get focused on a high level. You did great work, but now you need a break from writing.

Writing a book is like running a marathon. You just sprinted. You ran great, but now you need a breather. You can't keep up this pace forever. You need to recharge.

Let's work on the inner game of writing to help you get through the dip, fight resistance, and battle procrastination, which are inevitable parts of writing a book. Let's look at how to overcome your limiting beliefs.

BE ENTHUSIASTIC

First make sure you really, really, really want to write this book!

Are you enthusiastic about the book? Is it your life's purpose? Do you see how the book can help you reach your goal, whether that goal is making money, making the world a better place, or satisfying your ego? If you have a strong enough reason to write the book, you probably will finish it.

To paraphrase Rachel Aaron in her book *2K to 10K: Writing Faster, Writing Better and Writing More of What You Love,* if you aren't enthusiastic about writing the book, chapter, or example, then your readers certainly won't want to read it. She cuts scenes if she is bored when she edits her books. That's brave.

Your book does not have to be an all-encompassing encyclopedia on your topic. It should not include all the boring dribs and drabs of sleep-inducing trivia. You should fill your book with material that excites you so that your readers want to take action and follow your ideas.

I'M AFRAID OF RUNNING OUT OF IDEAS

This book shows you how to never run out of ideas! If you do these exercises, you'll have more than enough material. And you'll know exactly where to put each piece of information.

I'm Afraid of Feeling Like a Failure
When I Miss Big Goals

You might find setting small, achievable goals can help you. For example, if you say you will write for an hour a day, you might do that on the first day when you're jazzed up. The second day, you might write for 45 minutes. You might lie to yourself and say 45 minutes is almost an hour. On the third day, you'll work for only 15 minutes. You'll feel like a loser.

Big goals almost always create disappointment.

Instead, promise yourself you will accomplish an easy goal every day. Tell yourself you will write for *at least* five minutes. That's a ridiculously easy goal!

By doing that, you'll feel a sense of accomplishment when you put in your five minutes. That confidence will get you writing more and more. You'll write for 10, 20, 30 minutes, or longer. Some days more, some days less. But you'll get the book done, and you'll feel good about yourself when you do it.

If you can't write for five minutes a day, then hire a ghostwriter or coauthor, because you will not finish your book. Don't fool yourself.

"Consistency is more important than creativity," says David Nour, author of several books, including *Co-Create: How Your Business Will Profit from Innovative and Strategic Collaboration.*

You might benefit from using this template from my client Gary Patterson, author of *Million-Dollar BlindSpots©: 20/20 Vision for Financial Growth.*

The "million-dollar blindspot" preventing you from writing your book can be resolved when you write your answers on a three-by-five card about the **what** and **why** your book will provide.

For example:

I will write at least five minutes a day at 7:00 p.m. every day with accountability to my book coach to help me because I want to have a finished book I'm proud of.

I will_____

by_____

with support from/accountability

to_____

because_____

Download a printable version of this worksheet at
www.WriteYourBookInAFlash.com/worksheets

I'M AFRAID TO WRITE

If you haven't written a book, you might think writing is an exalted art form only the blessed few are good at. If that's holding you back, I have news for you: writing is a job. It's no different than any other job. They all require one key attribute: you have to show up for work every day.

People who say they aren't in the mood to write or have writer's block are fooling themselves. You don't wait for inspiration to write. You write and then get inspired to write more and more and more.

Do you think writing is a hard job? Look at the people who dig ditches. They probably don't like it, but they show up every day, even though it hurts. Cashiers who stand on their feet for eight hours doing the same thing over and over probably don't like that job either. But they show up every day, even though it is boring. Why should your writing job be any different? Writing is the best job you can have!

I'M AFRAID I'M NOT A GOOD WRITER

Your book is not supposed to rival Shakespeare. Your book needs to share ideas that help people. If you help a lot of people, they will think you write well.

People read your book to find answers to their most perplexing problems. They aren't expecting to read *The Old Man and the Sea*. Give yourself a break! Be interesting. Be factual. But don't obsess about being a Pulitzer Prize–winning author.

I'M AFRAID I'M A PERFECTIONIST

That's great! Your book gives you the opportunity to break this horrible pattern. It is impossible to create a perfect outline or first draft. It can't be done. Books are meant to be cobbled together piece by piece. As the creator of a new book, you have the freedom and flexibility to try ideas, test ideas, and use those ideas as springboards to better ideas. It also gives you the freedom to toss ones that don't work, don't resonate, or don't sing to your soul.

I'M AFRAID TO TAKE BREAKS OR MULTITASK

Some people advise you to have extreme focus and never let any distractions interrupt you. If that's your work style—great. However, I like distractions. It gives my mind a short break, and then I can focus again. Find what works best for you.

Think about your furnace. It turns on when it hits a certain cool temperature and works until it hits a desired temperature. Then it turns off. It turns back on when the temperature cools. If the furnace stayed on all the time, you'd waste fuel and money.

While this analogy is far from perfect, you might see validation in working when you're hot and stopping when you're not. You can take a short break to check email or balance your checkbook or rearrange your bookshelf. When you're done, go back to writing—refreshed and energized.

Taking breaks might not be bad if that's how you are wired. If that sounds like you, then I give you permission to stop listening to gurus who tell you to turn off your phone, stop checking your email, and stick to writing—no matter what. We're all wired differently, and if your mode is to take breaks, then do it. If you are hardwired to sit for an hour or two or three and be totally focused, then more power to you!

There's not one way that works for everyone. Do what works best for you. You don't have to listen to a so-called time-management expert who makes you feel bad because you answered the phone or checked in with your kids or did ten pushups to recharge your batteries.

Sure, there's a lot of evidence about the dangers of multitasking, but if you find you work better a certain way, then I give you permission to do it. Follow your own path. As long as you finish your book, it's all good!

I'M AFRAID MY GRAMMAR AND SPELLING ARE BAD

People might get writer's block if they are afraid of making mistakes with grammar, spelling, or style.

First drafts are usually awful. Even professional writers know they will have to spend time editing and revising. It's part of the process.

Don't let your fear of grammar slow you down. You can always hire an editor to get your book ready for publication.

I'M AFRAID TO MAKE MISTAKES

Mistakes are nothing to be afraid of. They show your readers you are human and imperfect.

Let's do a reframe. A reframe is where you look at something from a different point of view. For example, you might think yoga is weird. But if I told you every Major League baseball team uses yoga exercises, you'd probably think yoga is cool!

Let's reframe mistakes. Mistakes are actually cool because they show readers you aren't perfect. People don't relate to people who are perfect. Most folks think people who seem perfect are snobs, elitists, or nerds.

Readers want to relate to you. They aren't perfect. If they see you admit to not being perfect, they will be more apt to like you. If they like you, they will buy your book and tell their friends to read your book. They will hire you to work with them.

In fact, the first draft of this book was pretty bad. I didn't know it at the time, though. I thought I had a good first draft—until I read it!

Have I convinced you to show your imperfections?

I'M AFRAID OF PROCRASTINATION

Writing a book is easy. Worrying about writing a book is hard.

Many wannabe writers suffer from procrastination. You could read hundreds of books on this subject or get tips from thousands of articles online, but it all comes down to this: writers write.

Stop daydreaming and outline the book. After you finish the outline, write. Don't fall victim to the "getting ready to get ready" syndrome, or you'll never finish your book.

I'M AFRAID OF BEING AN IMPOSTER

It's not unusual for an author to suffer from a horrible condition known as Imposter Syndrome. Even highly successful people in business and education think they are not worthy of success because there is someone better out there.

If you are in an academic environment, such as a college, you quickly realize that no matter how smart you are, ten other people in your department can run circles around you. That doesn't mean you aren't smart. You can overcome this feeling if you present a rock-solid argument for your thesis. You'll know you are on solid ground.

Even Lin-Manuel Miranda, the creator of the hit Broadway show *Hamilton*, dealt with Imposter Syndrome. He said: "Anytime you write something, you go through so many phases. You go through the 'I'm a fraud' phase. You go through the 'I'll Never Finish' phase."

I'M AFRAID I'M A ROTTEN WRITER

Some people can't write and don't like to write. That's okay. You can still produce a book. Notice, I didn't say *write* a book. That's because you can dictate your book into a recording device. You can send the audio files to a transcriber who will turn the sound file into a Word file. Send that file to a ghostwriter or editor. You'll have the basis for your book. AI programs like **trint.com** will transcribe your entire book from audio to text for less than $100.

I'M AFRAID OF ISOLATION

Many would-be writers go stir-crazy because writing is a solitary business. Many people need external stimulation in the form of feedback and advice from a trusted authority. You can join a local writer's group, online forum, or connect with other writers.

I'M AFRAID OF TOO MANY COMPETING BOOKS

If you go to bookstores, libraries, or Amazon, you will find dozens of competing books. You could think the world doesn't need another book on your topic. You're wrong. There's always room for a new voice offering fresh insights.

In fact, readers love to buy several books on the same topic. Isn't your personal library filled with books on the same topics? Don't you know people who bought one diet book and then bought others because the first one didn't work?

Welcome to publishing, my friend, where there's always room for another good book.

HOW TO OVERCOME LIMITING BELIEFS

Here's a wonderful exercise to overcome limiting beliefs. It is based on NLP (neurolinguistic programming).

- Think of a limiting belief, and write it in the space below.
- Think of five reasons why this belief is not true, and write them in the spaces below.

Here's an example to get you started:

Limiting belief: I don't have anything to say.

Reason 1. This is not true, because I write a blog every week, so I must have something to say.

Reason 2. This is not true, because people respond to my blogs, so they must like what I say.

Reason 3. This is not true, because meeting planners ask me to speak, so I must have something worth saying.

Reason 4. This is not true, because whenever I make a comment about this topic in a meeting, people give me good feedback.

Reason 5. This is not true, because my blog readers ask me if I'm writing a book.

Now it's your turn.

Limiting belief: I...

Reason 1. "This is not true, because...

Reason 2. "This is not true, because...

Reason 3. "This is not true, because...

Reason 4. "This is not true, because...

Reason 5. "This is not true, because...

Here's another way to overcome limiting beliefs:

- Think of a limiting belief, and write it in the space below.

- Ask yourself, "What can I do to overcome this limiting belief?"

- Write five things you can do to overcome this limiting belief.

- Write the answers in the spaces below.

Here's an example.

Limiting belief: I don't have time to write a book.

Action step 1: I can wake up an hour earlier to write.

Action step 2: Instead of watching TV, I can write.

Action step 3: I can go to sleep an hour later and use that time to write.

Action step 4: I can write while I'm waiting for my kids to finish their soccer practice.

Action step 5: I can hire a ghostwriter or work with a book coach.

Your turn.

Limiting belief: I...

Action step 1:_____

Action step 2: _____

Action step 3: _____

Action step 4: _____

Action step 5: _____

Download a printable version of this worksheet at
www.WriteYourBookInAFlash.com/worksheets

These are actual examples from my book-writing seminars. People just like you have the same issues you have. By doing these exercises, you will bust those limiting beliefs that hold you back from reaching your potential to help people.

NEXT STEPS

In this chapter, you've learned how to let go of negative thoughts that hold back many writers. I hope you now have insights to identify and overcome those obstacles.

Hopefully your head is in the right frame of mind. Let's get back to writing.

You are about to discover the secret to writing your book in a flash. Hint: you probably learned this skill in high school.

Section II. Painting by Numbers with Words

Chapter 7

The Secret to Writing Your Book Fast

If you do enough planning before you start to write, there's no way you can have writer's block. I do a complete chapter-by-chapter outline.

—R. L. Stine

If you want to write the next *Glee*, why don't you do what their writers did?

Do you think they created the story on the fly? Do you think they came to work on Monday morning and said, "I wonder what predicament we can throw in this week?" Did you think they had winged it for so many years?

No way!

Here's their secret to writing a story that lasted more than five years with more than thirteen episodes per year.

They created the outline of their stories at the beginning. That's right. From the first moment bullies slimed Rachel with a Slurpee, the writers knew how the story would end. Rachel would get a starring role on Broadway, win a Tony award, fly back to Ohio, run into a classroom where her boyfriend, Flynn, was teaching, and tell him she was ready to get married.

Of course, you don't remember seeing that ending. It didn't happen. The actor who played Flynn died. The writers had to construct a new story ending—but they had a place to start from and points to hit along the way.

If one of the most-watched TV shows in the past decade relied on an outline, shouldn't you?

The outline gets you started in the right direction. If you discover new research, new stories, and new ideas, you can always change your outline and make your book even better. Your outline is a living, breathing document to help guide you to finish your book.

THE WRITING SECRET
EVERY HIGH SCHOOL ENGLISH TEACHER KNOWS

Did you know there is a secret formula to writing a business book? Once you know the formula, you will be able to write a book fast.

It's a secret every fast-writing author knows. It's also a secret your high school English teacher probably taught you. It's called writing an outline.

I guarantee you will write your book faster if you start by creating a highly detailed outline showing each chapter, each point, each story, and each action you want readers to take, think, and feel.

An outline is the skeleton of your book. Once you put all the bones in place, you have a solid framework for adding your ideas, thoughts, stories, anecdotes, facts, and figures. Like a skeleton, every bone of your book fits into a certain location. When it's in the right spot, you'll know. If something is missing or out of place, you'll know.

If you had a rotten English teacher who made outlines seem boring, I want to reframe your negative thoughts. You might think of your book outline as:

- A map of your next big adventure

- A giant to-do list of things you want to write about

- A business plan, where you own the business and keep all the profits

An outline is not a full description of your book. You don't have to explain anything in great detail. That comes later. Of course, if you are inspired, you can write as much as you like and create a detailed outline, but the point here is to list your ideas and put them in order.

WHAT IS AN OUTLINE AND WHY DO YOU NEED ONE?

An outline is a system to help you organize your thoughts and ideas. An outline helps make it easier for you to write your book. Plain and simple.

An outline is the road map to your book. You wouldn't think of driving anywhere without getting a list of all the roads and highways you need to take to get to your destination. The same is true with an outline for a book. A complete outline will be your road map to writing—and, more importantly, *finishing*—your book fast.

Here's what an outline looks like:

1. Things to Do in San Diego

    a. City

        i.   San Diego Zoo

        ii. Petco Park

        iii. Balboa Park

            1. Art museum

            2. Science museum

            3. Sports museum

    b. Beach

        i.   Mission Beach

        ii. Ocean Beach

        iii. Pacific Beach

        iv. La Jolla

        v.   San Elijo State Beach

        vi. Carlsbad State Beach

    c. North County

        i.   Legoland

A number or letter precedes each point or subpoint. Each time you add a new point or subpoint, the word processor will add a new letter or number in the proper sequence. If I added a section on things to do in Los Angeles, the word processor would begin with the number 2 and each item would follow as in the first example. If you move points around, your word processor will automatically revise letters and numbers. It's a lifesaver!

Here are more reasons to outline your book before you start writing:

SAVE TIME

Time is the most important asset you have. You can always buy another book, but you can't buy another minute. When you have an outline, you will never wonder what to write. You will write faster. You won't have writer's block. You'll have time to take your kids to the park.

SAVE MONEY

When you have an outline, you will save money because you aren't wasting other people's time. Lots of people—editors, publishers, publicists, advertising agencies—have planned their schedules around your delivery date. If you fail to deliver the book on that date, you could spend a lot of money in surcharges. Or your book might move to the back of one vendor's to-do list, which could delay book production.

WRITE FASTER

Let's say you can write 1,000 words a day without an outline, but *with* an outline you can write 2,000 words a day. Simple math shows you can finish your book in half the time!

If you take that concept one step further, instead of needing 60 days to write a 60,000-word book, you'd need only 30 days or even 20 days! Think of all the things you could do—personally and professionally—with those extra days.

GET FOCUSED

Is any problem worse than writer's block? Okay, heart attacks, strokes, and all sorts of illnesses, but you know what I mean. When you stare at a blank computer screen and have nothing to write about, that's terrifying. It's also demoralizing, frustrating, and time wasting.

However, those problems can be overcome with—you guessed it—an outline. An outline keeps you focused. When you start a writing session, you can instantly see what you need to write. The other great thing about that outline in terms of keeping you focused is you can *choose* what to write.

When you have an outline, you are focused on what you need to write.

YOU GET A FEELING OF ACCOMPLISHMENT

As you write, you can cross off items on your master to-do list. You'll get a sense of accomplishment. You'll know the end is in sight.

GET ORGANIZED SO YOU WON'T OMIT ANYTHING IMPORTANT

Wouldn't it be a shame to pick up your freshly printed book, turn to your great essay on your favorite topic, and realize you *forgot* to include it? That could happen if you don't have an outline. After all, your book will contain hundreds if not thousands of facts, figures, ideas, stories, and anecdotes. It is all too easy to forget something if you don't stay organized.

Most likely, you'll write in the early morning before your kids are up—or late at night after everyone's asleep. These might be the two worst times to write because you are not at your best. You could forget to include a funny story or a dire warning or a persuasive fact. Or you might forget to include a "thank-you" to people who helped babysit your kids while you were writing. Wouldn't you hate to have that happen?

BRAINSTORM

An outline helps you brainstorm because one good idea always leads to another! However, you might not get to that great idea without writing a few other ideas first. Writing and outlining gets your brain flowing.

It's like running. You don't start at a fast pace. You walk, then walk faster, then jog, then run. The same is true with writing and creativity. You must warm up first and put ideas on paper. Then you'll develop more ideas and better ideas.

Get Feedback

This might be one of the most important reasons to have an outline. It is easier for your peers, agent, and mastermind partners to review a three-page outline than a 300-page book. First, the outline is a quick read. Second, no one except your mother wants to read a rough draft of a 300-page book (Truth alert: Your mother doesn't want to read a lot of pages. She wants to see her name in the dedication and show the cover to her canasta friends.)

Seriously, outlines give these reviewers a quick-and-easy way to see what your book is about—and what is missing. They might have ideas you hadn't thought of and point you to resources and reference materials you didn't know about.

When you get feedback, you'll find some points are unimportant and should be cut. Getting feedback earlier rather than later means you won't waste time and resources writing and researching that topic.

Don't Become a "Pantser"

Figure 4: An outline helps make sure you don't paint yourself into a corner with no way out. (Images Provided by PresenterMedia.com)

If you don't have an outline, you will run out of ideas. Some fiction writers call themselves "pantsers" because they don't use outlines. Instead, they write by the seat of their pants. They start their novels with an idea, but they have no idea where the story will go.

While this might sound exciting to a nonfiction writer, there is a danger to this style. Sometimes pantsers create an implausible plot that has no resolution. Like a do-it-yourself handyman who literally paints himself into a corner, there is no way out. They've wasted their time and have to start over. If you value your time, don't be a pantser.

CASE STUDY: BETTY'S STORY

One of my clients had wanted to write a book for years, but she was stuck. She was good at telling people she wanted to write a book and at showing her passion for the topic. She couldn't wait to tell any new person she met about her idea for a book.

The problem? Betty was bad at writing the book. After months and months of telling people about her dreams of becoming a best-selling author, helping thousands of people, and leading a national movement for her cause, she hadn't written a word.

Betty had knowledge, passion, and vision. But she lacked focus. She couldn't focus on one idea at a time and put those ideas in a logical order so she could write.

A business colleague put us in touch. In our first working session, she told me the book would show people with disabilities how to lead productive lives. She was a case in point, as she overcame problems to lead a successful life, and she wanted other people to feel as empowered as she was. That's a good topic.

As logical as that sounds, she didn't present this information in a logical way. She was all over the place. But that was okay. I took notes and asked questions. Then I organized her thoughts into an outline, complete with chapter headings, subheadings, and placeholders to illustrate her stories.

I sent her the outline. She was delighted. She told me for the first time, she was able to get a handle on her story and could write the book.

She felt relieved because she had a road map to get to her destination.

THE OUTLINE PROCESS

When you finish, you'll have a living, breathing document to keep you focused, *and* it will adjust as you go. An outline doesn't lock you into things that no longer apply. As you write and research, you'll discover new facts and stories. That's great! You can include those new findings. You'll also find dead ends and theories that don't pan out. That's great too. Cut them.

YOU'VE CREATED A CHECKLIST WITHOUT REALIZING IT

After you finish the outline, print it, and use it as a visual checklist. You can easily see what you need to do. As you finish writing each item, you'll see how much progress you've made. It's a great motivator!

I'd guess many books don't get written because their authors got tripped up by something and never recovered. If you look at a book or outline like a paint-by-numbers kit that gets filled in piece-by-piece, however, you might feel more empowered. After all, in a paint-by-numbers picture, the smallest piece is as important as the largest piece. Everything needs to be in place.

NEXT STEPS

You need to create an outline to save time, save money, preserve your sanity, complete your book on time—and create a better book. Simply put, without an outline, you might run out of things to say.

Hopefully you are excited to start. Let's outline the book!

CHAPTER 8

OUTLINING THE TEN CHAPTERS

I believe that everyone has the ability to write a book.
Most would-be authors simply don't know where to start.

—Brian Tracy

Freedom is a wonderful thing. You can do anything. You can go anywhere. You have unlimited choices.

Your book could have 10 chapters or 20 chapters. It could have 2,000 words or 65,000 words. So many choices! That's where a lot of would-be authors get stalled. They don't know how many words, how many chapters, or how many "anythings" they need to put in their books. They don't even know when they are done!

Ah, but there's the problem with freedom: You have so many options, you don't know where to start. You procrastinate.

Let's give your book a solid structure so you can start. This chapter will show you what a typical book looks like. Once you know the basic format, you can adjust each item to suit your needs. When you have completed the exercise to create 10 chapters, you will also have created your table of contents! Your book is already taking shape.

BASIC BOOK STRUCTURE

Let's look at how to construct a nonfiction business book. Once you know the basics, you can tweak the model to suit your goals.

First, let's assume your book has 10 chapters.

You can have more or fewer. But 10 gives us a starting point. Chapters can be the same length or not. It doesn't matter.

CHAPTER OVERVIEW

Each chapter should have its own major theme. Ideally, each chapter follows a thought pattern that leads the reader to get to know, like, and trust you, so they adopt your ideas and want to give you their business. This is done via stories; anecdotes; visual elements such as charts, graphs, pictures or cartoons; essays; and quotes from famous people.

Every chapter should answer these questions:

- What is this chapter about?
- Why is it important for my reader to know this?
- How will I share my message?
- What will happen if readers follow my instructions? What will happen if they don't?
- What key ideas or action steps should readers remember?

This format will help a professional who wants to build their brand, urge people to adopt their point of view, or leave a legacy for people to follow. Of course, every book is different, so modify it as you see fit. This description should help you focus.

THE FIRST CHAPTER

Chapter 1 is the overview. You tell readers your big idea. The first chapter explains the problem you will solve. It presents a road map of what the book contains, and it explains why you are the best person to write the book. You could also lay out the book, by telling what the reader will learn in each chapter.

Do *not* go into great detail about all your wonderful ideas and processes. You can tell them what you will explore with them. But don't show them how to do it here. You do that later. You can promise them and tease them, though. Be inspirational (e.g., "You can do it!") and educational (e.g., "Here's what you'll discover").

CHAPTERS TWO THROUGH NINE

These chapters explain your basic premise and go into as much detail as needed to prove your points.

FINAL CHAPTER

The last chapter (in our example, chapter 10) summarizes your key ideas and shows actions readers can take. Ideally, for a business author, the next steps should include how you can help readers with consulting, speaking, coaching, or other services. Authors of a legacy book might list actions readers can take to further their careers, help the world, or come to peace with themselves.

ADDITIONAL MATERIALS

Books also have front matter (legal info, dedication, testimonials, preface, foreword, and table of contents) and back matter (index, bibliography, resources, and sales material).

HOW TO OUTLINE YOUR BOOK CHAPTER BY CHAPTER

Figure 5: Chapter outline for a book on leadership.

Enough theory. Let's outline your book!

Look at the daisy illustration, which shows the theme for a leadership book. Each chapter reinforces the author's ideas about leadership. In this case, you'll see 10 chapters that include an overview (chapter 1), a summary or next steps (chapter 10), and eight chapters that illustrate each major point. They are:

- Overview
- Courage
- Honesty
- Focus
- Respect
- Culture
- Supportive
- Humility
- Confidence
- Conclusion, Next Steps

BOOK OUTLINE FORMAT: ALL PURPOSE

Here's another outline you can use:

Chapter 1: Overview/importance of the problem you are solving

Chapter 2: History of the problem

Chapter 3: Current state of the problem

Chapters 4–9: Descriptions of problems and solutions

Chapter 10: Future

CASE STUDY: DAVID HORSAGER: AUTHOR, *THE TRUST EDGE*.

David Horsager is CEO of Trust Edge Leadership Institute, where the mission is to develop trusted leaders and organizations, and the hope is to make a dent in the global trust crisis.

David is the leading expert on trust and how it's built into everything from individuals and organizations to global governments. His work has been featured in prominent publications such as *Fast Company*, *Forbes*, the *Wall Street Journal*, and the *Washington Post*.

David has worked with clients ranging from Fortune 100 companies like Verizon and FedEx, to the New York Yankees and US Congress. He helps leaders and organizations become more trusted in their industry through research, speaking, consulting, and human capital development.

As best-selling author of *The Trust Edge* and *The Daily Edge*, he has taken this platform across the United States and onto six continents.

He invented the Enterprise Trust Index™ and leads the charge in one of the nation's foremost trust studies—The Trust Outlook™.

Here is the table of contents for *The Trust Edge*. Notice he added "parts" or "sections" to help readers focus clearly on his points. The first part sets the stage. The second part shows his unique perspective.

The other parts build on these themes.

Part 1: The Case for Trust

Chapter 1: The Trust Edge

Chapter 2: Impact of Trust

Chapter 3: Barriers to Overcome

Part 2: Eight Pillars of Trust

Chapter 4: Clarity

Chapter 5: Compassion

Chapter 6: Character

Chapter 7: Competency

Chapter 8: Commitment

Chapter 9: Connection

Chapter 10: Contribution

Chapter 11: Consistency

Part 3: Transforming Trust

Chapter 12: Extending Trust

YOUR TURN: LIST YOUR TEN CHAPTERS

You can outline your book by listing ten chapters and their themes on this worksheet. When you finish, you'll have your table of contents.

You could write only one or two words. That's fine. If you'd rather write a sentence, that's fine. Don't struggle to find perfect chapter titles. That comes later.

Fill in the lines below, and you'll take a giant step toward finishing your book.

Write your answers below:

- Introduction and overview_____
- Theme 1_____
- Theme 2_____
- Theme 3_____
- Theme 4_____
- Theme 5_____
- Theme 6_____
- Theme 7_____
- Theme 8_____
- Conclusion/Next Steps_____

Download a printable version of this worksheet at
www.WriteYourBookInAFlash.com/worksheets

NEXT STEPS

Congratulations! You've completed the first step in the outlining process—and you've created your table of contents. Unlike other writing coaches who tell you to "brain dump" your ideas from your head onto paper and organize them, I gave you structure to get you started. If you did a true brain dump, you would run out of ideas because there is no structure. You won't see what you forgot to include.

In my method, you have a system to guide and prompt you to move ideas from your head onto paper. You won't have that deer-in-the-headlights look when you follow my instructions.

You have created the outline for your 10 chapters. Let's create the outline for each chapter.

CHAPTER 9

OUTLINING CHAPTER ONE

Creativity is intelligence having fun.
—*Albert Einstein*

When your readers start reading the first chapter, their minds are filled with hope and anticipation. They think:

- What will I learn?
- How will I benefit from reading this book?
- What problem will this book help me solve?

Your first chapter must answer those questions. It sets the tone for the book and hooks readers. If your first chapter is a winner, readers will be more likely to finish the book. If your first chapter is a dud, they might put it back on the shelf and never look at it again.

As you can see, the first chapter is vitally important.

Readers like to see these elements in the first chapter.

BIG PROMISE

The first chapter makes a big promise to the reader. It shows them how their lives will improve by reading this book.

Readers buy your book for one purpose: to solve a problem. If you can show you understand who they are, what motivates them, and what keeps them up at night, you will earn a reader.

WHO YOU ARE AND WHY THIS IS IMPORTANT TO YOU

People want to read a book from someone they know, like, and trust. The first chapter helps you introduce yourself to them. Tell them your story.

- Why did you decide to write the book?
- Why are you the best person to write this book?

The answers will help build a bond between you and readers.

Here's a surprise alert: People like to see you are vulnerable and have made mistakes. People don't want to sit at the feet of infallible experts. They want to relate to people like them who have battle scars, who have tasted defeat, and who learned from their mistakes. Readers pay you to make sure they don't make the same mistakes.

ROAD MAP FOR THE BOOK

The first chapter can present an overview of the remaining chapters. That way, they can see your blueprint. There's a comfort in knowing where you will take them.

YOUR TURN: CHAPTER ONE OUTLINE

Answer these questions:

What is your big promise in chapter 1?

What big problem will the book solve?

How will this help the reader?

Why did you decide to write the book (your mission)?

Why are you the best person to write the book (your background)?

What is the road map for the rest of the book?

Download a printable version of this worksheet at
www.WriteYourBookInAFlash.com/worksheets

Next Steps

Now you have a good idea of how to start the book. It contains your big promise, a bit about you, and your passion for this topic, enough information to get the reader started, and a road map for the rest of the book.

Let's outline the middle chapters.

CHAPTER 10

MAKE YOUR POINTS: OUTLINING THE MIDDLE CHAPTERS TWO THROUGH NINE

I always have a basic plot outline,
but I like to leave some things to be decided while I write.

—J. K. Rowling

Chapters 2 through 9 prove your points. These chapters work to convince your readers you are an expert—someone they should hire—because they'll come to know, like, and trust you.

Each chapter has a Big Idea.

What is the Big Idea you want to get across in each chapter? You must answer one basic question: "Why is this important to the reader?"

Here are a few examples:

- To be a good leader, you must listen first.
- To get the best price, study the supply and demand for the product.
- To create an enthusiastic workforce, you must train people properly.

If you don't tell readers why they need to read the chapter, they won't read it.

PROVE YOUR POINTS WITH DESCRIBERS

In the assignment in the previous chapter, you created a theme for each chapter. Now you must convince your readers to your way of thinking. You do this by including proof to your chapter outline.

DESCRIBERS Prove Your Points

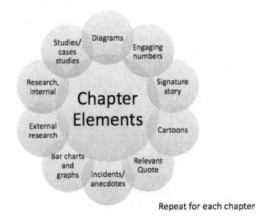

Figure 6: DESCRIBERS help prove your points to your readers. (Images Provided by PresenterMedia.com.)

DESCRIBERS is a mnemonic device I created to make it easy for you to brainstorm and identify information for each chapter. Each letter in "describers" stands for a word. Each word in this group identifies a technique for convincing people to come to your point of view. For example:

Diagrams

Engaging numbers

Stories

Cartoons

Relevant quote

Incidents/anecdotes

Bar charts and graphs

Every relevant question

Research

Studies and case studies

If your chapters use several of these elements, you will convince readers you are a thought leader and a person they want to know, like, and trust. You don't need to have all these elements in each chapter. However, if you use this device as a guide, you will never run out of ideas.

This description explains the tactics:

Diagrams are visual descriptions of your material. They can describe a process or a system.

Engaging numbers. Some readers will not be convinced by words alone. They want to see numbers that prove your points.

Stories can be long or short anecdotes. A signature story is a longer story that shows your purpose or mission.

Cartoons illustrate your points and might add humor. Use Google to find cartoon sites where you can pay the artist for the cartoon. It's important to ensure you have purchased the correct rights to use the work in a book (not a blog or advertisement). Keep the receipt to verify your rights to use the material.

You can also draw your own cartoons, even if you have little talent for drawing. See the cartoon below by consultant David A. Fields, author of *The Irresistible Consultant's Guide to Winning Clients*. His book contains many cartoons he drew to illustrate key concepts.

Figure 7: Figure courtesy of David A. Fields.

Relevant quotes can inspire readers to take action or to reflect on your ideas. You can find quotes on many websites, including **www.BrainyQuote.com**. When you search by topics, you'll find several interesting quotes to inspire your readers.

I'd suggest you use fresh references and quotes. Everyone has heard about Edison and his ten thousand lightbulb experiments, for example. Lots of quotes haven't been heard. Use them so you stand out. You don't need permission to use a quote of a sentence of two.

Incidents/anecdotes bring your points to life. People remember stories longer than they remember rules.

Bar charts and graphs illustrate numbers. They could show trends or projections. Word has many charts and graphs templates that are easy to use so you can create professional looking images.

Every relevant question from a frequently asked questions page might help readers understand your ideas. As an expert on this subject, people ask you questions. Here's your chance to answer those questions once and for all.

You might get additional questions if you post the following question to your followers on social media: "What is your biggest concern about [this topic]." You will get great content for your book and you will help those followers. It's a win-win situation.

For this book, I asked my e-zine readers to contribute their ideas. You'll see their names and ideas throughout this book.

Research you conduct and present will position you as a thought leader. You can do your own research or use work done by others. If you use other people's materials, cite them as the source.

Studies and case studies provide evidence to support your ideas by showing how other companies or people overcame problems.

CASE STUDY: DAVID HORSAGER AND *THE TRUST EDGE*

Throughout *The Trust Edge*, David Horsager uses these DESCRIBERS as proof points:

- Personal stories from his own experiences
- Quotes from famous people, including Vince Lombardi, Benjamin Disraeli, Colin Powell, and many others

- Case studies from famous people and companies, such as Walmart and Kmart, Google, IKEA, Warren Buffet, and others

- Research from books, magazine articles, and company websites, including *Harvard Business Review* and *Bloomberg BusinessWeek*

- Instruction and overviews

- Research reports with figures

- Information from other books (clearly noted and attributed)

- Summary of key points

Story Arc Format: Thought Leadership Model

Once you have gathered your material, you'll need to present it in a logical order. This suggested order can keep you on track. Of course, you can modify it to meet your needs.

Chapter title

Interesting quote

Main point

Story that describes it

Definition

How to attain it

Chart

Case Study

Research

What to avoid

Cartoon

Case study

Research

Assignment

Next Steps

STORY ARC FORMAT: THE HOW-TO FORMAT

The how-to format is a useful story arc. Henri Junttila, author of *Writing Blog Posts Readers Love*, describes this technique:

- Introduction (story if possible)
- What (define the concept)
- Why (why learn this)
- How (how to apply the information)
- What if (objection)
- Mistakes (blunders to avoid)
- Example (from my life or a made-up example)
- Takeaway
- Action steps

YOUR TURN: OUTLINE CHAPTERS TWO THROUGH NINE

Pick one chapter. Write the chapter number and the key idea for that chapter.

Make a copy of the following worksheet for each chapter. Use this worksheet to jot down ideas for as many DESCRIBERS as you can.

Key Ideas Worksheet for Chapter

	DESCRIBERS	Your idea
1	Diagrams	
2	Engaging numbers	
3	Story	
4	Cartoons	
5	Relevant quote	
6	Incidents/anecdotes	
7	Bar charts and graphs	
8	Every great question	
9	Research	
10	Studies, case studies	

These 10 blank spaces stare at you and cry out, saying, "Fill me up!" That might provide the kick in the pants you need to read more research reports or interview more experts.

Download a printable version of this worksheet at
www.WriteYourBookInAFlash.com/worksheets

When you do additional research, you'll feel much better, and you'll have a better book.

If you have a hard time creating 10 ideas, don't worry. I'll give you tips on how to do research. Remember, the more original content you have, the better. I'll also show you a technique for writing great stories.

CREATIVITY TIPS

1. After you finish each exercise, ask yourself, "What else?" That simple statement could help you think of another story, fact, or point. Keep asking "What else?" until you run out of answers. Then ask it again, five minutes later. Chances are, you'll think of something else.

2. Ask yourself, "Why?" This powerful question will help you think of additional elements to support your major points. The more times you ask "why," the more answers you will get.

NEXT STEPS

Each chapter contains a big idea or point you want to prove. You must provide enough evidence to convince readers. I call these proof points DESCRIBERS. You can use as many as you need to make your case. When you complete the exercises in this chapter, you will have plenty of content to use, and you will have almost finished the heftiest part of your outline.

Now let's look at the final chapter.

CHAPTER 11

OUTLINING THE FINAL CHAPTER

I couldn't write a book,
because there's no applause at the end of writing a book.

—Lin-Manuel Miranda

The final frontier—the last chapter.

You're almost done. In this chapter, you will:

- Summarize what you told them.
- Suggest next steps.
- Show how they can work with you.

SUMMARIZE WHAT YOU TOLD THEM

This chapter serves as the summary chapter. You can quickly and succinctly restate your key points and conclusions.

SUGGESTIONS FOR NEXT STEPS

You can help your readers best by showing them what they need to do next.

HOW THEY CAN WORK WITH YOU

As a thought leader, business consultant, and expert, you must show readers how they can work with you. If you don't do this step, you won't get new business.

You might think it is improper or beneath you to "sell" in your book. Let me help you get over that misconception. If you don't show your readers how they can work with you, you are doing them a disservice. After all, they spent many hours getting to know you and coming around to your way of thinking. They will wonder how they can work with you.

Can you help them consult? Speak? Coach? Do something else? They'll want to know.

If you don't tell them how you can help them, you will frustrate them. And if they hire your competitor because they didn't know what you did, you will be frustrated.

As business coach Patricia Fripp told me, "It is not your client's responsibility to remember you are still in business."

NEXT STEPS

Congratulations! You've done the heavy lifting. The next steps in the outline are easy.

CHAPTER 12

CREATING THE FRONT MATTER

I'm a great planner, so before I ever write chapter 1,
I work out what happens in every chapter and who the characters are.
I usually spend a year on the outline.

—*Ken Follett*

Before the first chapter, books contain these items:

- Testimonials
- Title Page
- Legal Information
- Dedication
- Foreword
- Preface
- Table of Contents

Let's look at each item.

TESTIMONIALS

A testimonial is an endorsement for your book. Testimonials might convince prospects your book is an excellent investment of their time and money.

Testimonials get the reader excited to read the book and show them your ideas should be valued because famous people respect your ideas.

If you have several pages of testimonials, you'll bask in the glow of the branding effect of these famous people. Readers think you are in the same league as those celebrities.

Get as many testimonials as possible. I've seen books with eight pages of testimonials. The more testimonials you get, the more you will impress prospects.

Testimonials can appear on the back cover of your book, in press releases, and on the book's Amazon page. Testimonials provide many benefits and uses.

What Makes a Testimonial Good?

All testimonials are not created equal. There is an art to writing a good testimonial.

Let's look at what makes a good testimonial.

- Short. Only a sentence or two because people like to skim. People might not read long testimonials. If you get a longer testimonial, trim it.

- Specific. Testimonials should either say *why* you are wonderful—"Dan's advice helped me win a $20,000 contract"—or why your book is wonderful—"This book will help novice authors write their books faster." No one cares that you are wonderful in a general sense—they want to know why your being wonderful will help *them*.

- Identifiable. Testimonials should include the person's complete name, title, and company. For example, "Dr. John Smith, director of pediatric services, Mayo Clinic." If you have an author buddy write a testimonial, it could have his or her name and the title of his or her book. For example, Jane Smith, author of *Write Now!*, never uses a testimonial with only the first name and initial of a person. It looks fake. For example, "Mildred P., of Canton, Ohio."

HOW TO GET TESTIMONIALS

It isn't hard to get testimonials, because people want to help you. Your "competitors" want to see their names in print. Celebrities in your industry want more exposure. The only thing holding you back from getting testimonials is your fear of failure. Ask!

HOW TO ASK FOR A TESTIMONIAL

What do you say to ask for a testimonial? Here's a polite and effective email I received from an author who sought my endorsement. You can model this email for your book.

EXAMPLE: TESTIMONIAL PITCH LETTER

Subject line: Hey, Dan! Can I send you a copy of my new book, *Future Marketing*?

> *Hi Dan,*
>
> *Hope you are well! So, my new book, Future Marketing, is coming out, and I'm looking for a few folks interested in reviewing the book on Amazon. I'd be happy to send you a copy (either paperback or Kindle version). Of course, you don't need to read the whole book...just a few chapters will give you the gist. ;)*
>
> *Interested?   More   info   on   the   book   here:* **futuremarketingbook.com**
>
> *Thanks! BTW, what's the latest with you? Anything I can help with?*
>
> *Jon Wuebben*
>
> *CEO, Content Launch*

I like this email because it is short and to the point. Plus, he shows an interest in helping me by writing, *"What's the latest with you? Anything I can help with?"*

Based on this letter, I thought he sounded like a great guy. I clicked through to his website, where I saw testimonials from people who are far more famous than I, so he gained credibility with me. I read about his book, which sounded interesting. I asked him to send me the book and wished him well. I wrote a nice testimonial and reviewed the book on Amazon.

Did you notice he offered to send the PDF version or a hard copy? Having that choice can save you money because a PDF is free. You'll spend $5 to $10 dollars to print and mail a book. A PDF is also more immediate. They can open it, read it, and write about it while the idea is fresh in their minds.

The other great thing about this pitch is that Jon notes I might not have time to read the entire book. That sentence makes it easy for the person to write a testimonial based on reading a small section. The easier you make it for people to give you a testimonial, the more testimonials you will get.

Jon told me he used LinkedIn and a tool called Green Box to email his contacts.

"It's amazing," he said. "It costs $170 to email all 5,0000 of my LinkedIn connections. I don't like doing that kind of thing, but you know what? It worked. I heard back from over 400 people! Crazy. Twenty-five hundred opened the email! Unreal.

"The email I wrote was magic too. Short and to the point. I used to write long emails—never again. They don't work," he said.

Be like Jon. Your colleagues want to help you. Make it easy.

TESTIMONIALS FROM CLIENTS

I'll bet you do great work. Congratulations! Your clients probably tell you how happy they are every day. Don't let their praise disappear.

When you speak with them, write their comments, and ask them if you can use that information. Offer to send the written version of their comments to them for their review and approval to use as a testimonial. They might add more details or add more glowing descriptions.

When clients send you emails containing words of praise, ask them if you can use their comments in your book. They'll be thrilled you honor them.

If praise hasn't been forthcoming, don't worry. Call your clients and ask them for testimonials. They probably won't know what to say, so

I'd suggest you ask one simple question: "How did you benefit from our products or services?" They'll give you specifics that will make a great testimonial.

For a play-by-play on how to do this, read the following case study.

CASE STUDY: KEVIN DONLIN

"Testimonials are a necessity. They offer proof your service or product actually works," says Kevin Donlin, author of **Marketing Multipliers: 11 Simple Tools to Grow Your Business**. "And, just like Krugerrands, you can never have too many."

How do you get more great testimonials?

Do three simple things: listen, write, and ask.

Specifically:

1. Listen for signs your clients love what you do.

Any time a client says anything nice about you, your ears should perk up like a dog hearing the UPS truck. This is your cue to…

2. Write what your client said, word for word, as best you can. Then…

3. Ask if you can use their comments in your marketing materials. Send an email like this:

"~Contact.FirstName~, thanks for saying that. I really appreciate it. Would you be willing to let me use your comments, with your name and company, on my website and other marketing materials? It would mean a lot to me. And it would tell others what to expect when doing business with me."

Nine times out of 10, your client will agree. Email their comments to them for confirmation, along with this note, which often prompts them to add more to their testimonial:

"~Contact.FirstName~, thanks again for agreeing to let me use your comments about my business. Below is what I think I heard you say on the phone today. Would you please add to or subtract from it until it says exactly what you want it to say, then send it back to me? Thank you!"

When you do those three things, you'll get testimonials like these:

"*Marketing Multipliers* is off the chain! I put up a winning Adwords landing page with your 'Hot Button Detector' strategy.... So far, it's outperforming my best converting control 35% to 22%—that's an increase of 59%!! Thanks a mil!"

—Daniel Barrera, CMC, Parkland, Florida

"*Marketing Multipliers* paid for itself *many* times over. I sent out six letters and received two full-price-paying clients. I would not have had them if I had not sent the letters using one of the templates you gave. Thanks a ton!"

—Dennis Neitz, sales trainer, Cottage Grove, Minnesota

TITLE PAGE

This page contains the name of the book and the author's name. It can include the publisher's name. John Grisham says this is the page authors should sign when they sign books.

LEGAL AND COPYRIGHT NOTICES

Every book has a legal disclaimer. You don't have to write this anew. You can copy it from another book or from the material below. It says three things:

- You own all the rights to the book, so don't copy it.

- You aren't making any promises that anyone who reads the book will become rich or healthy.

- If you are writing a fiction book, all characters are creations and bear no resemblance to real people, so don't sue me for libel if you think you are mentioned in the book. As a nonfiction author, you don't need to include this, but it is useful to know.

Copyright information is usually on this page. You can use this template as a sample:

Copyright © 2018 by Your Name

All rights reserved.

Printed in the United States of America.

No part of this publication may be reproduced or distributed in any form or by any means without the prior permission of the publisher. Requests for permission should be directed to **Your@emailaddress.com**, or mailed to Permissions, Your address.

Neither the publisher nor the author is engaged in rendering legal or other professional services through this book. If expert assistance is required, the services of appropriate professionals should be sought. The publisher and the author shall have neither liability nor responsibility to any person or entity with respect to any loss or damage caused directly or indirectly by the information in this publication.

ISBN-10: [insert number]

ISBN-13: [insert number]

Library of Congress Control Number: [insert number]

The [Title of Book] is a pending trademark [Your Name] (if applicable)

Your company name

Street address

City, State, ZIP code

DEDICATION

Thank your spouse, partner, kids, family, parents, or any special person who put up with you while you wrote the book. This is a special tribute, and it should be brief. Don't confuse it with acknowledgments, where you thank people who helped you create the book (i.e., agents, editors, researchers, and people who gave you moral support).

FOREWORD

A foreword is an introduction written by another person. It lends credibility to the book. The foreword, usually about 500 to 1,000 words long, could praise your work and the timeliness of the subject. The foreword comes before the preface. The foreword is not mandatory.

You might consider highlighting "Foreword by Famous Person" on the front cover and title page. Vint Cerf, a founding father of the Internet, wrote the foreword for my *Online Marketing Handbook*. Paul and Sarah Edwards, the married couple who have chronicled the work-at-home movement, wrote the foreword for my *101 Businesses You Can Start on the Internet*. Putting their names on the book covers added credibility to my books.

Note: "Foreword" is commonly misspelled as "forward." "Foreword" is correct.

PREFACE

The author can write a preface, which is a brief introduction. It could answer questions such as how this book came to be written, why you are the right person to write the book, how you found the information, and why people should buy the book.

It can include acknowledgments. However, if you have many acknowledgments, put them in the back in a separately labeled section to avoid boring readers.

The difference between a foreword and a preface is the foreword is not written by the author.

LIBRARY INFORMATION

This material helps librarians figure out where to shelve your book.

TABLE OF CONTENTS

The table of contents (TOC) is the master overview of the book. It contains each chapter's title and starting page number. Your word processor can create the TOC automatically if you use the outline feature in your word processor.

Here's a word to the wise: If you manually type the TOC, be sure this is the very last thing you do with your book, as page numbers will change as each editor or reader makes revisions. Even so, it's better to let your word processor or a professional populate the TOC for you.

NEXT STEPS

Wasn't that easy? It's like filling in the blanks. Let's move to an even easier part of the outline—the book's back matter.

Chapter 13

Creating the Back Matter

Writing, to me, is simply thinking through my fingers.

—*Isaac Asimov*

This material appears at the end of the book.

About the Author

You can write about your favorite subject—you! One or two pages is enough, even for a big business card book. In today's ultramarketing-centric world, you want to strategize what to write so readers want to take the next steps to work with you.

If your goal is to offer additional services to readers, include your business email address and website.

Consider adding your phone number if you want to talk to readers. Use a post office box instead of your home address to protect your privacy. If you have a publisher, don't use their address. They probably won't forward material to you reliably. You never know if they'll still be in business many years from now.

Bibliography

A bibliography list of sources for your book. You can include books, articles and links to online interviews, podcasts, websites, and resources.

The **Chicago Manual of Style** explains the correct style.

INDEX

An index is an alphabetical list of names and subjects in the book. An index is a useful tool to help readers find information quickly. Many books today do not have indexes.

ADVERTISING MATERIALS FOR YOUR COURSES, COACHING, PRODUCTS, ETC.

Rick Frishman, founder of **Author101University,** says, "The book is the business."

He means you won't get rich from selling books. Most authors sell fewer than 500 books.

However, smart authors write books to build their businesses. Business executives use books as "big business cards" to build their reputations, establish themselves as experts, and launch their careers to the next level.

This section could display your ads or one-sheets describing services you offer, such as courses, training, and consulting. It's your book. You are the king of your book. You can do anything you like.

FOR KINDLE BOOKS, ASK FOR A REVIEW

You can—and should—ask readers to review your book on Amazon. Many e-books use this tactic.

SAMPLE REVIEW REQUEST FORM

Here's an example from Tom Corson-Knowles, founder of TCK Publishing:

ONE LAST THING...

If you enjoyed this book or found it useful, I'd be very grateful if you'd post a short review on Amazon. Your support really does make a difference, and I read all the reviews personally, so I can get your feedback and make this book better.

If you'd like to leave a review, then all you need to do is click the review link on this book's Amazon page here: **amzn.to/yourlink (direct link to the "Create a review" page on Amazon)**

Thanks again for your support!

Note: To get the link, you must first upload your book to Amazon's marketplace. When your book is live, get the review link, insert it into your book, and reupload your book.

NEXT STEPS

Congratulations! You completed your outline.

You'll see spots where you need more information. Let's look at how to find it.

CHAPTER 14

DRAWING ON RESEARCH: FILLING IN THE BLANKS

There is no substitute for face-to-face reporting and research.

—Thomas Friedman

If you're like most people, your outline has gaps. That's okay. You don't need to have all the facts in your head; however, you do need to know how to find information.

When I was a student at Northwestern, a professor told me the purpose of the university was not to show you what to think but rather how to find information so you can think.

Consider yourself a detective who hunts for missing facts.

CASE STUDY: A TALE OF TWO BOOKS

When I wanted to write a "big business card book" to show myself as a thought leader on publicity, I gathered my notes and wrote **Reporters are Looking for YOU!** in several days. You could have locked me in a room with no other resources, and the book would have flowed from my head because I knew my material cold.

When I wrote the book **Business Speak** for publishing giant Wiley, however, the writing situation was the exact opposite.

The year was 1999. Voice recognition was a new technology.

I thought it would be the hot new technology, and I'd sell a zillion books as businesses tried to figure out how to add voice to their products. After all, phones were getting smaller, and people would have a hard time typing on them, right? We can speak. Why should we be limited to a keyboard to interact with phones? I thought it was a winner.

So did my publisher. They gave me a nice contract to write a 200-plus page book.

Since I was not an expert on this topic, I interviewed companies using the technology, researchers creating the tools, and analysts covering the field. I used my journalism skills to research and write the book.

Let me tell you, it was a hard book to write. Back then, few companies used voice recognition technology. It wasn't until 2015 or so that Siri and Alexa made voice recognition a mainstream application.

I found only a handful of companies using voice. I couldn't find enough case studies and reports and interviews to fill more than 100 pages. I was at my wits' end. I couldn't find anything more to write about.

I told my acquisitions editor I'd return the advance. She refused. She said I *had* to finish the book!

I persevered. It actually was a pretty good book after all!

For this book, I used a combination of writing skills. Part of the book flowed from my brain to my fingers to the computer, based on my personal experiences. Other sections came from interviews I conducted, seminars I attended, and material I found on the Internet.

Which way is best? It doesn't matter. Some thought leaders write books from their heads and quote only themselves. Other business executives quote other people to validate their ideas. In fact, some people became thought leaders because they assembled information from other people. They are the thought leader because they have all the information and sources of information at their fingertips. Malcolm Gladwell, author of **The Tipping Point** and other true bestsellers, interviewed people for his books and drew his own conclusions.

THE HOTEL ROOM TEST

If I locked you in a hotel room for a week, could you write your book off the top of your head? Would you have enough ideas, examples, stories, and other evidence to write the first draft? Or would you scratch your head after a few hours and admit to yourself that you need to talk to other people and read other sources to finish your draft?

Maybe yes, if your book is based on your personal experiences and insights.

If you are a true thought leader, you might have all the information in your head. Those ideas can flow from your brain to your fingers to the computer.

I want to relieve you of a terrible burden shared by many authors. They think they need to know it all when they start writing their books.

Not true.

You can get additional information in many ways. In fact, getting additional sources helps prove your points because readers will see other people support your ideas.

Good authors want to cite other sources and find out what they don't know.

Legal Considerations Concerning Research

Do not copy other people's work and pass it off as your own. That's called plagiarism. If people realize you are plagiarizing someone, you will lose their respect, and you could be sued.

Here's what you can do legally and ethically. You can quote two or three lines of text as long as you attribute the information to the person. This is called the doctrine of fair use. Put the words in quotes, and list the person's name and where it was published.

If you paraphrase the quote, you should still use the person's name. For example, "The Bureau of Labor Statistics showed unemployment dropped by 0.7 percent in April."

If you aren't sure about whether to use material, consult an attorney who specializes in publishing.

Quoting Experts and Other Sources Make You Look Good

"Interviews produce a lot of content and articulate the same things you are saying in different ways, bringing clarity. Besides, they bring credibility to your book and act as champions," said Luis Zorzella, one of the authors of *Revenue Growth Generation: Four Proven Strategies*.

FREE RESEARCH TOOLS AND RESOURCES YOU CAN USE

The Internet offers many free tools you can use to find new material.

GOOGLE

Google should be the starting point for your research and for your brainstorming. You can find anything you need to find by typing a word, phrase, or name.

Additionally, Google is a wonderful tool for brainstorming additional topics. I'll show you how to use Google's power in a way you might not have known. Let's say you are writing a book about service dogs. By searching Google, you'd find this information:

- Ads for service dog companies and how to register a service dog.

- Organic listings for service dog companies, articles about service dogs and sexual abuse survivors, a map of your local area that has service dog businesses, and articles about service dogs.

- At the bottom of the page, you'd see links for how to get a service dog, service dog sales, service dogs for PTSD, service dog types, and service dog laws.

This information is solid gold. You might get ideas you hadn't thought of, sources to review, people to interview, and sites to quote.

Also, don't limit your search to Google's first page. There's plenty of great material on the following pages, according to Joan Stewart, publisher of the *Publicity Hound* e-zine.

"I also look past page one of organic search results. You never know what you'll find buried on pages two and three," she says.

If you'd like to find resources that most people don't know about, use Google Scholar, which has academic listings and research papers generally not found in regular search.

But don't stop there. Look under the "news" tab. You'll see news articles and company press releases.

Search Engine Notification Services

Google Alerts helps you stay current on events about your topic. This free service delivers news about your topic to your inbox. To get started, go to **www.Google.com/alerts** and fill out a simple form that asks for topics you want to cover, your email address, and how frequently you want to receive updates.

Wikipedia

Wikipedia is the world's largest encyclopedia. Wikipedia gives you new insights. It has facts and figures to prove your points. However, some academics don't trust Wikipedia as a reliable source, because there is little control over the editorial review process. If you use Wikipedia for initial research, check other sources to ensure accuracy. You can start this process by going to the bottom of the Wikipedia page and clicking the source links used to write the article, and then digging deeper from there.

Amazon

Amazon is another amazing source of information about your subject area, your competitors, and market research for your book. Let's look at these topics.

Information about Your Subject

Amazon has every book in your field. That's a valuable research library for authors. You can read short summaries of books to find out what they cover. You can read about authors and decide if you'd like to interview them or ask them to write reviews or testimonials. Many books display their table of contents and first few chapters, so you can learn more about their scope.

HOW TO FIND COMPETITORS' BOOKS

Amazon can show you competing books and bestsellers.

To find books in your field, go to Amazon, and type the name of a book that competes directly with yours. In this example, I've typed the name of one of my books, *Reporters Are Looking for YOU!* Scroll to the section on the page called "Product Details." You'll find various publishing information, such as date and ISBN numbers. You'll also see "Amazon Best Sellers Rank." Right below that is the good stuff. Amazon tells you which category the book is in. My book is listed in "Public Relations." No surprise!

Product Details

Paperback: 90 pages
Publisher: CreateSpace Independent Publishing Platform (February 9, 2012)
Language: English
ISBN-10: 1466345004
ISBN-13: 978-1466345003
Product Dimensions: 6 x 0.2 x 9 inches
Shipping Weight: 4.8 ounces (View shipping rates and policies)
Average Customer Review: ★★★★☆ (13 customer reviews)
Amazon Best Sellers Rank: #3,539,346 in Books (See Top 100 in Books)
   #1705 in Books > Business & Money > Marketing & Sales > **Public Relations**

Now click on the link for "Public Relations," and you'll see the real juice of this exercise. You'll see a page with three important pieces of information.

*Figure 8: Read Amazon's Best Sellers list to find books
that compete with yours.*

First, you'll see the top 100 books in this category. That's important because you will see what is selling and what people are interested in. Second, in the far-right column, you'll see "Hot New Releases." While the main list might be dominated by classics that have been top sellers for years, this new list shows you newcomers that attract readers.

Right below new books are "Most Wished For" books. This gives you additional insight into books people are buying.

For all three topics, you can click on links to see more titles. Now you know how to find your book's competitors. You'll also know where to tell Amazon to index your book.

Don't stop there.

Do this same exercise for other books in your field. You might find those books are indexed under different categories. You might find a more suitable category. You'll find additional competing books.

Note: This example does not work on mobile phones. Use a desktop computer or tablet to see results.

Review the Table of Contents

Amazon displays the table of contents for many competing books. You are not reading this material to steal. You read it to be inspired and to add your point of view.

Read Amazon Reviews of Other Books and See What Readers Think Is Missing

Read all reviews. You'll find what people like in the bestsellers as well as what they thought was missing. That's the gold you are looking for. You can include these new ideas in your book—and point out your book is better than others because it has this information.

Goodreads.com is an excellent site that offers in-depth reviews from readers.

SKIM COMPETING BOOKS

Some authors have posted the first few pages or the first few chapters of their books on Amazon. You can read the first 10 percent of any e-book on Amazon for free using the "Look Inside" feature. Just click the book cover on the book's sales page on Amazon or click "send a free sample."

RESEARCH COMPETITORS

Find five best-selling books that compete with yours. Study them. See how they persuade and inform readers. Of course, don't use their stories. Instead, make notes about what you like and what you don't like. You are not copying them; you are using them as a basis for improvement. By discovering limitations of competing books, you can create a unique book that adds more value to your readers.

YOUR CLIENTS

Who knows your readers' problems better than your clients?

"Ask your clients for their challenges, and then write and develop great content related to them, and provide them your insights to cover these challenges," said Chad Barr, president of the Chad Barr Group and founder of the Digital Empire Academy.

INTERVIEW EXPERTS

You should interview authorities. They give your book more credibility. Readers like to see other experts validate your points.

Quoting people is a great way to build your network. They might help promote your book or introduce you to other experts who could provide additional information.

INTERVIEW INSTRUCTIONS

Would you like to conduct meaningful interviews? I learned these tactics when I worked as a daily newspaper reporter and business newspaper editor—as well as the author of eleven books.

INTERVIEW TIPS

First you have to secure an appointment. People are busy and might not want to talk to you; therefore you must show them why it is in their best interest to talk to you. You might point out you will quote them by name, title, and company. If they are authors, you will print their book titles and put links to their sites or their books on Amazon. Assure them you will not steal their work, and you will make them look good. Yes, experts are concerned about how you will represent them.

Record the interview using free software like Zoom. The recordings will allow you to review the interview to make sure you accurately quote them, and you can even publish the videos (with permission) on your website, YouTube, or even as a podcast. **Here's a quick tutorial video on how to use Zoom for interviews.**

When you talk with them, follow these tips:

- Call or arrive on time.
- Ask for permission to record the session.
- You call them, not the other way around.
- Ask them how much time they have—even if you confirmed the time before. It shows you respect their time.
- Remind them how they will benefit by talking to you.
- Write your questions in advance. Don't wing it, because you might sound disorganized. You can always ask more questions during the interview.
- Ask easy questions first and difficult questions last. The easy questions make people comfortable. They will start opening up to you and will offer more insightful answers. If you ask questions that are more challenging too early, they might get defensive or shut down.
- You may or may not want them to review what you write. Pro: they can spot errors or correct miscommunication. Con: they might be very picky and revise to the point of distraction. They might take a long time to get back to you and upset your schedule. If you let them review your work, ask them to return their comments by a certain date.
- Offer to send them a copy of the book.
- Ask them for a testimonial or a review if you have built rapport with them.

ASK GOOD QUESTIONS

Good questions start with "how" or "why." These are open-ended questions because experts must provide detailed answers.

The opposite of this is a close-ended question, which can only be answered "yes" or "no." For example, "Do you think people should eat cheese?" The expert answers "yes" or "no" but offers no explanation. If you ask, "Why do you think people should eat cheese?" you'll get an answer with more detail and opinion.

WHAT DO YOU WANT TO LEARN?

Don't ask questions for the sake of asking questions. Focus on information your readers will find interesting. If you don't, they'll stop reading. Chances are, if you are interested in the topic, your readers will be too!

In 1998 I thought Internet security would be a good topic for a book. Of course, I'm not an expert on the subject, so I interviewed dozens of experts for my book *Risky Business: Protect Your Business from Being Conned, Stalked, or Blackmailed on the Internet.*

Many experts were happy to offer information. They gave their time and advice graciously. Of course, no one asked to be paid. They realized their missions were to educate the public—and getting free publicity never hurts.

Don't be afraid to send emails to university professors or to researchers at think tanks. The latter want to get quoted because your book gives them more credibility, which helps them build their personal brands. The bigger their brands, the more they can charge their clients.

You actually help your sources, so don't talk yourself out of contacting big names and important people. They need you as much as you need them.

Blog Posts, Articles, Podcasts

Read and listen to other thought leaders in your field. You can find interesting insights and sources to support your theories. You might want to interview these people so your book has even more credibility. Reading and listening to these materials could open a wide range of experts for you to invite into your community. You might help promote each other's works.

The value of doing research is that you'll find what the world knows. Add your insights to those thoughts, so you are even more valuable to your readers and clients.

To find these sources, go to Google and type:

- Blogs about [my topic]
- Articles about [my topic]

Podcasts

You can appear as a guest on podcasts. Hosts might ask you questions you might not have thought of. You might also think of different ideas because you are in a different environment, and you are using a different part of your brain.

To become a guest on a podcast, go to Google and type "podcasts on [my topic.]" You'll see lists of podcasts. Check out each website and listen to a few episodes to see which ones fit. You'll also get a feel for the interview style. Send an email to the host and tell them how their audiences will benefit from your message. For information about how to be a guest on a podcast, read Jessica Rhodes' book, *Interview Connections*.

YouTube

Many people have posted short videos on YouTube that can teach you how to do almost anything. By typing questions into YouTube's search engine, you could find professors or other experts who give insights into your topic. You can cite these sources and use them in your book. Or you could reach out to those experts and interview them for additional ideas.

TED Talks

TED Talks are influential videos from expert speakers on virtually any topic you can think of. Search the TED Talks database, and you might find a professor or a respected researcher who can share new insights.

College Course Catalogs

If colleges teach your topic, you might find instructors' course outlines and descriptions. You could read those to generate new ideas. Or you could interview professors.

Online Courses

Experts teach thousands of course on online course sites like Udemy and Coursera. You can glean information for free by looking at lesson plans and course outlines or you could pay to take the course.

Many courses are free, but others can cost several hundred dollars. Here's a way to—possibly—get them for the price of a few cappuccinos. Register on the site to join the expert's mailing list. They might have promotions, offers, and discounts. I've taken several classes for $10 on Udemy, even for courses with a list price over $200.

Competitor's Blogs, Speeches, Slide Share, LinkedIn, and Testimonials

Read your competitors' content to see what topics interest their followers. Your readers and clients are interested in the same information. You should also monitor their testimonials because you might find clues about things to write about. Usually you find this information on their websites and LinkedIn profiles.

Speeches and Presentations

People post presentations on LinkedIn, Slidebank.com, and BrainShark.com.

Newspapers, Magazines, and Trade Journals

News and articles offer ideas and insights into new trends. They can also make you aware of thought leaders and case studies.

Local Libraries

As wonderful as the Internet is, don't overlook your local library. Research librarians could turn you on to resources or give you access to expensive databases not available on the Internet, such as Lexis/Nexis and eric.gov.

Q&A Forums

LinkedIn Groups

People ask questions in LinkedIn groups. You can review those questions and provide your own unique answers. You can post questions and use answers in your book.

Quora.com

Quora.com is a free, open forum, where people ask questions about many topics. You can search for your topic, and you'll probably find questions people have asked as well as answers people have submitted. This could be a good source of material. It is useful for brainstorming too. Of course, you can add questions and learn from answers people submit.

Client Questions

Perhaps the best research tool is questions your clients ask. After all, your clients are ideal customers for your book. If they asked you a question, chances are, people just like them have the same questions.

Also, ask your customer support staff to send you questions people ask. Finally, search your email for their questions.

BE ORIGINAL

I can't tell you how many people write books about leadership, sales, motivation, diet, and fitness that contain the same tired anecdotes, facts, and inspirational quotes. This is lazy writing, if not outright plagiarism. If you plan on telling people they should practice something for 10,000 hours to become a master or they should drink 64 ounces of water, think twice. Draw on your original ideas, so people will think of you as an original thought leader, not a thought repeater.

Figure 9 101 Businesses You Can Start on the Internet was translated into Portuguese.

CASE STUDY: WRITE YOUR BOOK WITH INTERVIEWS:*101 BUSINESSES YOU CAN START ON THE INTERNET* BY DAN JANAL

Many of my clients say they don't have time to write a book. I completely understand. After my first book was published by a professional publisher, I asked my editor if he'd be interested in another book called *101 Businesses You Can Start on the Internet*. He loved the title and told me to write the book—fast—because the next big trade show was 90 days away. He wanted to show buyers he had a manuscript ready to be published.

My original thought was I would have a lot of time to write the book and fit it in while I was doing my day job of publicity. But I knew I couldn't do 101 interviews in just 90 days. That would equal more than one interview every day for 90 days.

That doesn't sound hard for an experienced writer like me, but you have to realize there's a lot of work that goes on behind the scenes to get the interview in the first place. You have to find suitable businesses, find the right people to ask, set appointments to interview them, interview them, transcribe interviews, and edit transcripts. That's a lot of time. If I had six months—180 days—it would have been hard, but doable. Having only 90 days made the task seem impossible.

I love solving problems. How could I make this work? This idea came to me: I'd find companies and ask if they wanted to participate. If they did, I'd send them a questionnaire. They'd complete it. I'd edit it.

Then I tweaked it one step further. I included the questionnaire along with the request.

This worked.

Not only did I have enough material for a book, but since all questions were the same, readers could see how people in different industries responded. There were similarities and symmetries to the process that made the information easy to access.

The book was such a success that two things happened. First my publisher asked me to write a sequel, *101 Successful Businesses You Can Start on the Internet;* then a publisher in Brazil bought the rights to the book for his country and published it.

NEXT STEPS

If you use these ideas, you'll find so much information, you won't ever have to worry about having enough details for your book.

In the next chapter, let's find out how to turn your research into compelling reading with stories.

CHAPTER 15

ADDING COLOR WITH STORIES

Information travels under the guise of what seems like idle chatter.

—*Jonah Berger, marketing professor,*
Wharton School, University of Pennsylvania

Your outline provides the sturdy bones that hold your book in place. DESCRIBERS (see chapter 9) provide the muscles holding bones together. Stories are the skin that brings your message to life.

Your background might not include storytelling as a means of communication. Or you might come from a world of numbers (e.g., charts and graphs), or a world of commands (e.g., dos and don'ts) or a world of processes (e.g., do this first; do that second). Those are fine ways of communicating in certain situations. And certain people learn by certain methods, so you should definitely use these instructional methods at the right time.

However, I strongly suggest you use stories as well because:

- People like to read stories.

- Readers are moved by stories.

- Stories persuade people.

- People remember stories.

Let's pretend you want to convince people to use chainsaws properly. You could admonish them to use tools carefully. You could cite statistics showing the number of deaths and accidents chainsaws cause. Will they follow your advice based on your logic? Maybe. Maybe not. They come across so many facts and figures every day.

But long after they have forgotten facts and figures, they'll remember this true story my bookkeeper told me:

"My neighbor went to church one Sunday, but her husband said he was going to stay home. He wanted to trim tree branches. When she came home, she didn't see her husband in the house. She went to the back yard and found him dead on the ground with blood all around him. His chainsaw had bucked and sliced off his leg. He bled out before the ambulance could arrive. My advice to you is: You don't have to be an expert in everything. Hire a professional. Your life might depend on it."

Now do you think your readers will pay more attention to your step-by-step instructions?

That's the power of a story—power you can't get from statistics or facts alone.

Stories teach, demonstrate, convince, warn, gain trust, show your personality, build rapport, and add humor.

Stories don't have to be long. The chainsaw story contained about 100 words. Yet it had a beginning, middle, and an end. It also made a point. Your stories should have a moral, prove a point, or teach a lesson. In this case, the lesson was: "Hire a professional. Your life might depend on it." The moral of your story could be your sales message or your call to action.

You might think, "I'm no storyteller."

Fortunately, it is easier to create stories than you might think. Although dozens of techniques work, the case-study formula always works. You can read about other story formats in **Persuade with a Story** by Henry DeVries.

CASE STUDY OUTLINE FOR BUSINESS STORIES AND INSPIRATIONAL STORIES

Structure Outline

1. Describe the problem in detail. Make it as painful or heartbreaking as possible.
2. Show what they did to try to solve the problem. But explain this solution didn't work.
3. Then they hired you.
4. You offered this solution.

5. Show what happened. (i.e., now he doesn't have the problem.) Describe how wonderful his life is now.

6. Lesson learned. (i.e., If you do this, you could have the same result.)

Example 1 (Simplified)

1. Joe had agoraphobia. He was cut off from all the fun in the world, and he sincerely missed being with people.

2. He tried listening to hypnosis tapes to overcome his fear, but they didn't help.

3. Then he hired you as his coach.

4. You told him about service dogs.

5. He got the dog. Now he can go outside and meet friends, shop in a store, and get exercise.

6. Because he got a service dog, Joe now leads a productive life.

Example 2

1. Amy's company had a problem measuring their sales metrics.

2. They were losing sales and didn't know why. They were losing money and were about to lay off people.

3. They hired our company to survey the situation and offer solutions.

4. Our company reviewed the situation and offered specific solutions.

5. By following our company's advice, Amy's company increased sales by 200 percent.

6. Instead of laying off people, they hired more people and gave them raises.

Aim for between 250 and 500 words per story as a guide.

Dan Janal and Michael Hauge

STORY LESSONS FROM HOLLYWOOD STORY EXPERT MICHAEL HAUGE

Would you like your stories to be as dramatic and emotional as a Hollywood movie? Michael Hauge, one of Hollywood's top coaches and story experts, has worked with countless screenwriters, novelists, and filmmakers on projects starring (among many others) Will Smith, Morgan Freeman, Julia Roberts, and Tom Cruise.

I met Michael when we both spoke at a book marketing conference hosted by Indie Publishing International. Michael shared his 6-Step Success Story™ formula and permitted me to share it with my readers:

Michael Hauge's 6-Step Success Stories™

- *Setup—The "before" picture of your hero's everyday life. Select either yourself or a successful client as the hero. Picture details of this hero's life before encountering you, your product or your process. Create empathy through conflict: sympathy, jeopardy, likability and/or a special skill. Reveal how your hero is emotionally stuck or tolerating a bad situation.*

- *Crisis—The event that moves the hero to action. In response to this new event, the hero will define a problem to be solved. Your hero asks questions and explores options, and establishes a visible goal he or she must achieve.*

- *Pursuit—The hero begins employing your process or product. Show details of at least two steps your hero takes. Include the ways you guided your hero to success. This gives potential customers the emotional experience of working with you and applying your principles.*

- *Conflict—The source of emotion in your story. Show us the obstacles and fears your hero was able to overcome by using your system. These are obstacles and fears your potential clients already anticipate, so including them will increase their desire to work with you.*

- *Climax—Vividly portray your hero's movement of success and victory. Detail the moment your hero crossed the finish line and achieved the visible goal. Include physical and emotional reactions of your hero and the reactions of loved ones.*

- *Aftermath—The "after" picture of your hero's new life. Show your hero reaping the rewards of working with you to accomplish the goal. Match the qualities of life your potential buyers want for themselves.*

"Now write the story, including these six steps," Michael said. "Then rewrite it, adding dialog and detail to bring it to life and create a 'movie' in the minds of your audiences or readers.

"Stories are all about eliciting *emotion*," he added. "Potential clients and buyers put themselves into the story by empathizing with your hero. Then they feel themselves achieving success as your hero does. In other words, with a good story you're giving them the emotional experience of working with you—and winning."

For more information, please read Michael's book *Storytelling Made Easy: Persuade and Transform Your Audiences, Buyers and Clients—Quickly, Simply and Profitably* or visit his website at www.StoryMastery.com.

YOUR TURN: CREATE TEN STORIES OR ANECDOTES FOR EACH CHAPTER

When I taught the Dale Carnegie class on human relations, "How to Win Friends and Influence People," I shared one of Carnegie's most important points with every class: The best way to overcome fear of speaking is to fill your head with examples and stories. If you have plenty of both, you'll never run out of things to say. That's a good rule to follow when you write your book.

I'd like you to create 10 stories for each chapter.

Having 10 blank spaces on paper or on a screen will force you to create. For example, if I said, "What are ten reasons you should pack an umbrella in your suitcase?" you might think of two or three reasons. For example, I want to protect myself from rain or extreme sun.

If I asked you to think of two more reasons, you might be stumped. I am. But then my brain goes into overdrive. I think, "To use as a self-defense weapon in case I get attacked." Or, "To use as a crutch in case my knee pops out." Granted, those things are not likely to happen, but you can see where an umbrella might come in handy.

If I have to think of six other ideas, I will stretch my creativity. I might think of stupid things or crazy things. I'm forcing myself to think differently. That's where the best ideas come from.

I know a copywriter who writes 50 headlines for each ad. Why? The first ones are good. Usually the middle ones are fair. But the final ones are brilliant. He uses those.

You won't get to the brilliant material if you don't slog through the mire first. The creative process works that way. Frankly, I think it is fun, and I hope you think so too.

Use this space to brainstorm 10 stories.

Download a printable version of this worksheet at
www.WriteYourBookInAFlash.com/worksheets

Story idea --Moral/lesson/point

1. _____

2. _____

3. _____

4. _____

5. _____

6. _____

7. _____

8. _____

9. _____

10. _____

WHERE DO YOU PUT A STORY OR CASE STUDY?

Case studies can start a chapter or follow an essay or exercise. The more stories you have, the better. Everyone loves a good story.

NEXT STEPS

Stories put the skin on the bones of your book. Now let's see how to make your book shine with great writing and layout, so you can write your first draft.

SECTION III. MAKE YOUR BOOK SHINE

CHAPTER 16

THE ART OF WRITING, EDITING, AND REVISING

The research is the easiest. The outline is the most fun. The first draft is the hardest, because every word of the outline has to be fleshed out. The rewrite is very satisfying.

—*Ken Follett*

Remember that paint-by-numbers kit we talked about in chapter 1?

If you've done the exercises in this book, you should have your outline ready. In reality, it is a giant paint-by-numbers kit for your book.

All you have to do is fill in the blank spaces, and you'll have your first draft.

The beauty of the outline is it is a visual representation of your progress. As you fill in the blanks, the picture becomes clear.

In this chapter, you'll see how to put words to your outline to construct your first draft. You'll also see how to revise and edit your work, because a first draft is *never* perfect.

THE FIRST DRAFT

The most important part of the first draft is getting it done. It doesn't have to be perfect. It doesn't have to look pretty. It doesn't even need to have all your facts and stories. It just has to get done.

Completing a first draft is a major accomplishment. You should be proud when you see it rolling off your printer.

Put it aside for three days, and then reread it with a fresh view.

If you're like me, you'll be surprised to see what you forgot to include. Chapters that seemed to flow when you first wrote them may need to be reorganized. Don't get discouraged.

The great thing about seeing holes is you will see where to fill them. This is all part of the writing process.

Anne Lamott, in her classic book about writing, **Bird by Bird,** said all first drafts are "shitty first drafts." I agree. Once you have a first draft, you can clean it and polish it. But without that first step, nothing happens.

First Drafts Are About Ideas, Not Perfection

Let's make the book-writing process as easy as possible. After all, writing a book is a long, tough process that taxes even the most skilled writers and subject matter experts. Why make it more difficult than it needs to be?

This chapter will help you get ideas out of your head and help you polish your writing without boring you with petty details of grammar and punctuation.

When Do You Write the First Chapter?

This is a tricky question! You could write it first. That way, you have the road map in front of you. You can update it as you learn more information after doing more research.

Some people look at the first chapter as a big hurdle—and they never overcome that hurdle. If that sounds like you, I give you permission to write the first chapter whenever you like. If you think chapter three is an easy chapter to write, start there. Do anything to get going.

Readers don't know where you started your book or in which order you wrote the chapters. They only care that they get value from the finished product.

Make the process easy on yourself. Write the book in the order that works best for you. You don't have to write in a linear (start to finish) fashion.

TONE

Write like you speak. Your writing should not sound like a PhD wrote it. You don't want your book to read like a dry academic journal. I know people who have advanced degrees who struggle to make their books *not* sound academic.

Have a conversation with readers. After all, when people read, they have a dialog in their minds. They read, but their brains think: *Is this true? Is this funny? Do I agree?*

Be yourself when you write. Your unique voice will make you and your book stand apart from thousands of competitors. When a prospect calls you, they'll feel as if they know you. If the book's tone and voice is different from the way you speak, prospects will feel disconnected from you. Your tone gives you the unique opportunity to help readers get to know, like, and trust you—the three essential ingredients in winning new clients.

TENSE

In my book-writing seminars, people ask me if they should write in the present or past tense. I tell them it doesn't matter *if you are consistent.* If you change tenses, voices, or point of view, you'll confuse readers.

THE SOUND OF WRITING

Where you work can have a big effect on your productivity. You might like to work in a quiet room. Or you might crave being around other people and working in a noisy room. That's probably why so many people use Starbucks as a second office.

You might listen to music when you write. After all, people who run or work out get motivated by listening to songs with strong beats and fast rhythms, such as *Eye of the Tiger* or *Flashdance.* Why shouldn't you? I like to listen to Bob Dylan's *Greatest Hits, Volume 1* and the Rolling Stones' *Greatest Hits, Volume 1.* Tim Ferriss not only listens to music, he listens to the same album over and over, *and* he plays the same movie in the background as he writes.

I'm giving you permission—as if you need it—to listen to music, watch a movie, hang out at Starbucks, or lock yourself in a quiet room if that's what it takes to get you to write. It's all good.

WHEN IS THE BEST TIME TO WRITE?

It depends.

If you work a nine-to-five job, you might be able to write only when you come home, and then only after you put the kids to bed. Some people wake up early to write for an hour before going to work.

You might find your biorhythms are more in tune to writing during the morning or evening.

Try different things and do what works best for you. Everyone is different, so don't compare yourself to anyone. There is no right or wrong way. There is *your* way.

WORK WITH DEDICATION

Writers write. Set a time and a goal each day. If not, you will be one of those people who say, "I will write a book one day." Or worse, "See that bestseller? I could have written that book."

DO BOOKS NEED TO BE WRITTEN FROM BEGINNING TO END?

I want to liberate you from the horrible misconception you have to write your book in order, from chapter 1 to the final chapter. That trap in thinking causes writers never to get started because they see the beginning of the journey, but the end looks so daunting. Or they dread writing a certain chapter, so they give up in the middle of the process.

As your book coach, I give you permission to write any chapter or story (or section of a chapter) in any order you like because you might get stuck on chapter 1. Remember, chapter 1 is where you provide the big overview, and you deliver the big promise and the big picture. Frankly, it is a big deal, and it can be intimidating. If that's the case, why not take it easy and write something easy? You'll find that is a liberating experience.

Or you could write the first chapter first because you'll have a wonderful plan to follow. Or you could write the first chapter last because you might revise the book when you discover new information. Or you could write it whenever you feel like it. It's your book. You're the boss. There is no right way, and there is no wrong way. The reader (and your editor) only care the book is done.

How Long Should Each Chapter Be?

That depends on what you want to say. A six-by-nine-inch book that is between 165 and 200 pages could have about 40,000 to 50,000 words in total. A big business card book could have 20,000 words and about 150 pages. Divide those numbers by 10 chapters to get an approximate word count per chapter.

This advice is not set in stone. It is a guide to help you. It is a recipe that will work. But like any recipe, you could add a few of your ingredients to make a wonderful book that satisfies your soul and meets your readers' needs.

Capture All Your Ideas Wherever You Happen to Be

Creativity is an odd beast. You never know when you will have a good idea. I strongly suggest you carry a little notebook, so you can write ideas as they occur.

You will not, I repeat, *not remember* that insanely great idea in five minutes if you do not write it down. You must write your ideas as you get them. If you are driving, pull over to a safe spot and then write your idea.

You should get a small notebook—not a scrap of paper—and carry it everywhere you go.

But don't get just any notebook.

The notebook should be small enough to fit into your pocket or purse. That's because if it is convenient to carry, you will take it everywhere you go. You will not carry a large notebook. Any small notebook will work. Moleskine, Field Notes, or a cheapo no-name brand from Target will suffice.

Unless you love writing in journals, I would not recommend a journal-sized notebook, because they are big and hard to carry around comfortably.

When you start a new writing session in front of your computer, take your notebook and transfer your ideas to your manuscript. Your notes will help you kick-start your next writing session.

You may want record voice notes with a free app that works with your smartphone or mobile device.

WRITING IN YOUR SLEEP

Have you ever had a great idea in the middle of the night? Many creative people do.

In fact, the idea could be so powerful, it wakes you up. But you probably turn over and say, "I'll write it in the morning." When morning came, you forgot your idea. Sound familiar?

You must capture your sleepy-time brainstorms.

If you're like my friend author Amy Jauman, you grab your pencil and write your idea on a notepad on your bed stand. When you wake up in the morning and look at your notes, you'll see this:

Figure 10: What was Amy thinking at 3:00 a.m.?

Can you guess what Amy wrote?

If you saw the word "video," congratulations.

If you dream and get a great idea, turn on the light and write your idea in your notebook. Then reread it. If you follow this simple plan, your note will look like English, with words and sentences. You might be tired in the morning, but your note will make sense.

CREATE YOUR OWN VOCABULARY

Thought leaders create their own lexicon and terminology. You might remember I did this with the word DESCRIBERS.

To turn your ideas into a word people can remember, use an anagram-creator tool such as WinEveryGame.com.

You type the first letters of your words (i.e. *S* for Story). The tool shows you words they form. If you run into a problem with difficult letters like *Q*, put an adjective in front of the offending letter. That's why I used "interesting quotes" instead of "quotes."

WRITE, THEN EDIT

Jean Feingold, author of *The Benefits of Concrete Block Homes,* told me: "Don't edit while you write. Writing and editing are two different activities. Just keep writing as long as ideas come to you. When you reach a stopping point, go back, run spell-check, correct any grammatical errors, and repair any holes in your thinking. This first edit is only designed to fix the rough edges. You will do many more edits before your book is ready for people to read."

BACK UP YOUR MANUSCRIPT

I back up everything. Every day. Some people are lazy and don't back up their work. That's the worst thing they could do (or not do).

Your hard drive will crash. It's not a question of "if" but a matter of "when." When that happens, would you rather copy a file from your thumb drive or tear your hair out (or worse)?

Here's how I backup my manuscript. Yes, there is a smart way and a dumb way.

The dumb way is to copy the file. Simple, but dumb, because you run the risk of overwriting a file or backing up a file that could be corrupted because computers can malfunction.

You want to have at least two backups. You have today's version and yesterday's version. You can't do that if the files have the same name. Name your file "Your Book and date," for example: *Flash 4-10-17.doc*. The next day, open the file in Word, and save it to the current date, i.e. Flash 4-11-17.doc. Copy files to Dropbox, Google Docs, a cloud-based server, or a thumb drive. You can also email a copy of the file to yourself. You'll sleep better knowing you have multiple backup copies.

THE IMPORTANCE OF SETTING DEADLINES

When I was a reporter for the *Today* newspaper in Cocoa, Florida, I had the rare opportunity to take the VIP tour of NASA's Kennedy Space Center as they planned the first space shuttle. It was a big deal. In fact, President Jimmy Carter took the same tour the week before. All the reporters from my newspaper walked inside mission control and saw the flight screens and computers.

After the tour of the launch pad and other facilities, we met in the press briefing room, where NASA's public information officer was ready to answer questions.

The first question came from our aerospace writer, a great reporter named Dick Baumbach. He asked a simple question, yet it was a question that took us by surprise. The conversation went something like this:

Dick: What are the chances of the space shuttle launching on schedule?

Public Information Officer: About 30 percent.

Dick: So that means there is a 70 percent chance the shuttle will not launch on schedule, correct?

Public Information Officer: Yes.

Dick: So why do you have a date you know you will probably not make?

(Dan: Here's the kicker. Pay attention.)

Public Information Officer: If we have a target date, all our suppliers will have a date to shoot for. If we don't have a date, they'd never deliver. We certainly do expect some vendors to miss dates. That's okay. We have built that into the schedule.

Sure enough, NASA didn't launch the shuttle on the target date.

The point of the story is to show that if you don't have a deadline for your book, it will probably never get done. A thousand good reasons will delay your book (got sick, kids got sick, vacation, holidays, bored, not inspired, lazy, ugh).

If you have a realistic and achievable deadline, however, you'll have a better chance of completing your book.

If creating a deadline is good enough to launch a rocket into space safely, it's good enough for you to write your book.

EDITING TIPS

Editing—especially cutting useless words—is a vital part of editing. Fearlessly cut words if they don't add anything.

I realize it is hard to cut any of your lovely words you worked so hard to write, but if deleting a thousand words would make your book better, you must do it. Don't mourn the loss of those thousand words. Your readers won't miss them.

Sometimes I'm prouder I *cut* a thousand words than I am when I have written a thousand words.

A good editor could probably trim 2 to 3 percent of your words without you even realizing it. They have an eye for removing "deadwood," a term for useless words.

I cut more than a thousand words—about 2 percent of the total—from this book's first draft simply by searching for items in my editing checklist in the next section.

EDITING CHECKLIST

My favorite editing tips, which I learned when I worked as a newspaper copy editor, are:

- *"That" can usually be removed. If it sounds good without it, you're set. If it sounds awkward without it, keep it (e.g., "Here is* another outline format that you might find useful." Remove "that," and the sentence reads fine).

- "The" can be cut sometimes. (e.g., "Which book will help the most?" "Which book will help most?")

- "The" can be cut if it refers to a noun, and you can make the noun plural. (e.g., "The book will help." "Books will help.")

- A prepositional phrase starting with "of," could be rewritten (i.e., "the title of the book" becomes "the book title.")

- Prepositional phrases using "of" can be deleted sometimes. (i.e., "Each of these tasks." "Each task.")

- Is/are and a verb ending in "ing" can be changed to the verb form only (i.e., "He is cutting trees." "He cuts trees.")

- Usually you can cut these words: very, now, just, only, and even. Read the sentence without the word. See how it looks. Hear how it sounds. If it sounds good, then cut the words.

You'd be surprised how many words you can trim.

You can listen to my free webinar on how to cut words. Go to **www.WriteYourBookInAFlash.com/flashbonus**

*Figure 11: Chip away anything that does not fit into your book.
(Images Provided by PresenterMedia.com)*

Proofreading Tips

No matter how many times you read your manuscript, typos will slip by. These tips will help you find typos:

- *Use the spell-checker.*

- *Read the text from right to left.*

- *Listen to the text via a text-to-speech app.*

- *Read the text out loud.*

- *Print out the manuscript and read it on paper instead of on a word processor.*

When I proofed this book, I used a text-to-speech app. I was shocked—and embarrassed—to hear hundreds of mistakes. My spell-checker did not and could not tell me when I left out an article, such as "a", or if I used "even" when I meant to write "event." But the app told me loud and clear. I'm glad I used the app before I showed the manuscript to anyone. Readers would have thought I was illiterate.

Linda Popky, author of **Marketing Above the Noise**, told me when she copyedits her clients' books, it is not unusual to make more than 3,000 corrections. She warns authors not to hire inexpensive copy editors from countries where English is not the native language, as those editors are likely to *add* mistakes to your manuscript.

After you've proofed it three times (on the computer, on a printout, and listening to it on a text-to-speech program), show it to a copy editor or proofreader.

Editors

Several types of editors can help you create your finished manuscript. You'd work with them in this order:

- *Developmental editors work with you as you write your book. Your book coach could also play the role of a developmental editor. They are concerned with your big ideas and the flow of the book. They might move paragraphs or rewrite entire sections of the book.*

- *Line editors take your finished manuscript and edit for context and content. They also look for word choices, badly written sentences, clichés, and style.*

- *Copy editors fix typos, punctuation, and grammar.*

Everyone—and I do mean *everyone*—needs an editor. You couldn't possibly find every typo and error. You don't know every nit-picking grammar rule or *The Chicago Manual of Style* either. Editors make you look better, make your readers happier, and ultimately help you sell more books. Plus, you'll learn how to become a better writer when you see how a professional editor wordsmiths your work.

REVISING

To make the revising process easier, I follow this system.

- *Buy three-hole punched paper and a loose-leaf binder with a clear insert cover.*

- *Print the manuscript and assemble it in the binder.*

- *Print a cover sheet and put it in the cover slot.*

- *Go to your favorite editing spot, such as a coffee shop or library. Don't edit at home or the office. By going to a different location, you'll look at your work differently. You won't have normal distractions (hopefully).*

I print books on three-hole punch paper. Here's a tip to save paper: print one page first, so you can see where to position the three holes. I learned that lesson the hard way.

Print a cover sheet and put it in the clear-cover flap of the binder, so the book looks real. Whenever you talk about your book, you can show people the binder. You are no longer a wannabe who talks a good game and never produces anything. You have a draft. Don't worry, no one will ask to read it.

REVISE WITH PEN AND PAPER

You can and should edit your book on the computer screen, but there's only so much editing you can do that way. Besides, when you see your work on paper and grab a pen (or pencil, in my case), a different part of your brain is activated, according to copywriter Kevin Donlin, author of *Marketing Multipliers: 11 Simple Tools to Grow Your Business.*

You'll find different errors, and you'll notice things didn't flow as easily as you thought.

You'll see what's missing or is in the wrong place. Believe me, you won't find those same items when you read a computer screen.

THE LAST MILE

Have you heard the term "The Last Mile?"

It started with the telecommunications industry. The phrase refers to the fact it is relatively inexpensive and easy to lay cable from the main station to the substation. But to get the cable the last mile to your office or house is expensive and difficult.

The last mile for an author is the hardest part.

In the last mile, you check your sources, verify links, look for typos— and lose sleep over wondering if you've said too much or not enough.

Relax.

It is part of the journey.

FEAR IS A POSITIVE INDICATOR

Fear is the truest indicator something is wrong. Fear is your gut telling your brain your instincts are right. When you are afraid, you need to fix something.

In my case, I had an upsetting feeling chapter 1 was not quite right. After several nights of tossing and turning in my bed, I reviewed it. I trusted my gut and turned one very long chapter into three easy-to-read chapters.

What are you afraid of?

THE NATURAL FLOW OF IDEAS

Coffee takes time to percolate.

Likewise, your ideas need time to grow.

That's why it is absolutely normal to have a crummy first draft. The great ideas you think about at this stage couldn't have come to you if you hadn't written the outline and rough draft first.

You will continue to have ideas—when you sleep, when you work out, when you day dream. Incorporate those new, great ideas. You'll even have ideas two seconds after you send the book to your publisher or to CreateSpace. Hopefully your publisher will understand and will allow you to update the book. There comes a point where the publisher can't change anything without incurring a cost. Be respectful. CreateSpace allows you to update the book any time you have a new idea. Do it. So you can continually revise your book.

NEXT STEPS

You now have dozens of tips to help you write and edit. Let's see how to get feedback.

CHAPTER 17

FEEDBACK

Writing on a computer makes saving what's been written too easy.
Pretentious lead sentences are kept, not tossed.

—P. J. O'Rourke

No one likes to hear bad news, but I'd rather hear bad news from a friend than from my publisher—or Amazon critics.

Book coach Mark Levy did his client a favor when he told her: "You don't have a 300-page manuscript. You have a thirty-page manuscript written ten times." Oops.

Mark Victor Hansen, cocreator of the *Chicken Soup for the Soul* series, told dozens, if not hundreds, of people to read and grade each potential story. The authors depended on feedback from their target readers to find the best stories.

Spencer Johnson, MD, said he revised *Who Moved My Cheese?* more than a dozen times after it was published as he received feedback from readers. He wasn't satisfied to rest on his laurels, even though the book sold more than 20 million copies.

You can get feedback from two great sources: your peers (peer review) and from your ideal readers (beta readers). This chapter will show you how to get the most from those people so your book goes to the next level.

PEER REVIEW

How do you know if your ideas are solid? Ask your peers—mastermind partners, colleagues, professors, and even competitors (although I prefer the term "co-opetition"). They will challenge your assumptions and tell you what you got wrong or left out. Hearing their comments can be brutal, but your book will improve after this review. You don't pay them. One day, you'll return the favor and review their books.

BETA READERS

When you feel confident about the quality of your book, you can show it to beta readers. Beta readers are volunteers who read a draft of a book and give their honest feedback on what works, what doesn't work, and what is missing. They differ from a peer review. Peers are experts who look for technical flaws. Instead, beta readers are your target readers.

Beta readers provide an invaluable service to authors because they offer unique perspectives authors don't have. Authors, after all, aren't the target reader. Beta readers want to learn and have their questions answered. If they don't understand something, they will tell you.

For example, my beta readers told me about boring case studies, exercises that weren't clear, and over-the-top self-promotion. They also told me what they liked!

"Beta readers are scary because they will criticize the words you poured your heart into creating. Do it anyway. One chapter never got glowing reviews from beta readers. After numerous tries, I cut the chapter. No one's missed it. Ironically, it was the sample chapter that won me a book deal from four publishers," said David A. Fields, author of ***The Irresistible Consultant's Guide to Winning Clients***.

Don't show the book to beta readers while it is in rough shape. You'll waste their time. Send the book when you have taken it as far as you think you can go. Readers will show you how much further you have to go.

WHAT DO YOU WANT BETA READERS TO DO?

Beta readers need direction. You must give instructions to beta readers.

- *What do you want them to do?*
- *What kind of feedback do you want from them?*
- *When do you need to have the manuscript returned?*

For example, you might ask if the stories prove the points, if chapters appear in the correct order, or if material is irrelevant. Of course, you can ask them what information they think is missing.

I've noticed four kinds of beta readers:

- *A content editor who will point out what doesn't work or could work better. They will make additional comments to improve the flow (i.e., chapters or sections that should be moved higher or lower) or will suggest additional topics or exercises.*

- *An average target reader. They will read the book as a normal reader would and will give you general impressions. They will find typos and will point out what they liked or see one thing they didn't like. Don't expect to make major improvements from these readers. You will get lots of feel-good notes you can use in testimonials.*

- *A copy editor who will spot typos and style errors. They aren't pros, though. They won't find all the typos.*

- *The fourth type either won't read the book or will read it superficially. They started with good intentions, but life interrupted them. That's okay. Thank them and ask for a testimonial based on what they read.*

There is no right or wrong reader. All feedback is good.

One thing I would do differently: I wouldn't send the book to all 10 readers at the same time. I'd send it to a few readers, wait to hear comments, and make edits. Then I'd send the revised version to other readers. There's no point in having 10 people show you the same error.

Ask them how they would like to receive the manuscript (i.e., printed copy by mail, Word file, or PDF via email). Create a double-spaced file or printout, so they have room to write comments. Surprisingly, all my readers asked to see the entire book. I would have been thrilled if they said, "I'm busy, but I'll read a chapter. Send one, and I'll read it." You might offer your readers both options (a chapter or the entire book), and let them tell you which they prefer.

WHAT DO YOU DO WITH COMMENTS FROM BETA READERS?

If they made comments you don't agree with, take a deep breath, and ask yourself, "Are they right?" Revise accordingly.

CASE STUDY: ACQUIRING AND MANAGING BETA READERS

You might wonder how to attract and manage beta readers. Author David A. Fields shares his three-part email sequence for beta readers that he used for his book **The Irresistible Consultant's Guide to Winning Clients**. You can modify this system to suit your needs, of course.

FIRST LETTER TO BETA READERS: INTRODUCTION AND RECRUITMENT

Hi, Dan.

You're receiving this email because (among other things) you've read my blog fairly often over the past six months, and that makes your opinion especially important to me.

And now, I have a favor to ask. My new book is scheduled to come out very soon, but there's still debate over the title. (Yikes.) If you would be willing to participate in a brief survey to help me find the right title, I would be hugely grateful.

The survey is anonymous, so I won't know whether you participated, but I hope you will.

The survey is at this link: [link]

Finally, I am looking for a handful of beta readers who would be willing to read through an advance copy of the book in a short period of time (about one week) once it's ready. If you're interested, please send me an email to let me know.

Thanks in advance for your help in naming the new book.

Best Regards,

David A. Fields is...

Managing Director of the Ascendant Consortium,

Author, *The Executive's Guide to Consultants*

SECOND LETTER: INSTRUCTIONS FOR BETA READERS

Note: Include the chapter the beta reader was asked to review.

Thank you for agreeing to preview parts of my new book. Your feedback will be immensely valuable.

I've sent you an excerpt of the book, and I've also included the introduction, so you can understand the overall layout of the book and how the excerpt you have fits in.

It's important to me that every part of *The Irresistible Consultant's Guide to Winning Clients* is packed with practical, useful tips, avoids the filler that plagues so many business books, and is a good read.

Therefore, please use the red pen I've provided liberally.

- Blah blahblah...blah blahblah.... Blah blahblah...

- Circle or underline or mark phrases, sentences, and sections you think are noteworthy.

- Yadayadayada... yadayada... yadaya yadayada

- Scribble out, x-out, or mark phrases, sentences, and sections you think are boring or add no value.

- There's a wide, right margin for comments. Comment away.

Plus, at the top of each page, I've placed a six-point scale to judge whether the book kept your attention or not. When you flip the page, please circle one of the points on the scale before you continue reading.

It's possible your packet includes some "bonus" pages. This is content I've removed to make the book shorter (and easier-to-read) and planned to make available online. *Let me know whether it should stay out or if it's a must to put back in.*

That's it.

I've included a pre-paid envelope to send back your marked-up pages.

PLEASE MAIL THE EXCERPTS BACK TO ME BY <u>JULY 15TH</u>!

Thanks again. I'm glad you're contributing to the book.

THIRD LETTER TO BETA READERS (INCLUDED WITH COPY OF BOOK)

February 27, 2017

Dan Janal

Address

City, State, Zip, Country

Hi, Dan.

Enclosed is your (first) copy of *The Irresistible Consultant's Guide to Winning Clients*. Your input during the beta-draft phase was very important and helped make the book much better than it would have been otherwise.

Of course, I hope you enjoy the book and find it helps your practice grow.

Two quick questions:

- **Would you please write a review on Amazon.com?** The following URL will take you to Amazon, where you can write a review: **WinClientsNow.com/review**

- Would you be willing to help create some visibility for the book? If so, please just shoot me an email saying you will.

Thank you again for your help, input, and support of this project. Enjoy the book, and, as always, if there's any way I can be of help to you, don't hesitate to reach out.

Warm Regards,

David A. Fields

NEXT STEPS

You've gotten feedback on your book. It's a rewarding and a humbling experience.

Next, we'll look at how to dress up your book so it looks great.

CHAPTER 18

DESIGN SECRETS THAT WILL MAKE YOUR BOOK A PAGE-TURNER

Design is a funny word. Some people think design means how it looks.
But of course, if you dig deeper, it's really how it works.

—*Steve Jobs*

Your ideas are valuable. But if people don't read your book, then your ideas are not worth anything to anyone. As much as we think our words shine, graphic artists tell us differently. The layout makes words more palatable. Fortunately, you can take the first steps in designing your book. These ideas will help you communicate your ideas to a book designer.

These tips will make your book look easy to read.

MAKE YOUR BOOK SKIMMABLE

People like to skim. That was true when I was an award-winning daily newspaper reporter and business newspaper editor nearly 30 years ago—and it is truer today.

Long blocks of text intimidate people.

That's why newspapers use short paragraphs and lots of white space to make articles look easier to read.

Smartphones and tablets have shrunk the reading space to a few inches—about the size of your palm. Small screens make even short messages look like a long book. Need I repeat that people today have short attention spans?

Fortunately, several writing and design devices can help you capture and keep your reader's attention.

They are:

- Italics

- Callouts

- Quotes

- Mnemonic Lists

- Numbered Lists

- Bulleted Lists

- Checklists

- Flow charts, Diagrams, and Process Visuals

- Infographics

- Cartoons

- Charts and graphs

- Pictures

- Subheads

- Assignments

- Summaries

ITALICS

Italics are the *slanted* typeface. You'll see many instances in this book. I didn't put them in. My sainted copy editors did. They know a good tool when they see one! Italics set the words apart from the main text, but don't stand out like a blaring "see me" that all capital letters would. Subtle. Very subtle.

CALLOUTS

Callouts are short blocks of text—perhaps a few words or a sentence at most. They appear in the middle of a page and use a larger font. A box or a colored background could set them off.

A callout highlights a thought or quote from your main text, so it stands out in people's minds. It also highlights your most important learning points.

Don't use more than two callouts per chapter, though.

Quotes

Beginning a chapter with a short inspirational quote from a famous person delights readers. It also looks good. Quotes, which can be italicized, use different type faces and are set flush right, so they break up the black wall of text. Print quotes after the chapter title and before the first paragraph. Use a different font than the main text.

Bulleted Lists and Numbered Lists

A bullet or a number can precede a list of items or instructions. Lists are fantastic devices to use because they:

- Break long blocks of copy
- Share information quickly
- Eliminate long sentences
- Add white space, which increases readability

Do you see how easy that was to read? Imagine if that text were one long sentence. It would be boring and more difficult to understand. That's why lists work.

Numbered lists should show readers how to accomplish a task in a certain order (e.g., "Follow these five steps to give proper feedback.") or when you refer to several items, such as, "You will learn these five things."

One problem I often see with lists is when words are repeated. That can cause readers to lose interest. You might hit the wall when it comes to creating unique and interesting verbs. After all, you can't say "learn" over and over again. Here are great words to use in a list. Speaker coach Lois Creamer, author of **Book More Business: Make Money Speaking**, offers these variety of choices to add versatility to your lists.

You will learn how to:

- Identify target markets—the quickest way to grow your business

- Qualify prospects faster and more effectively

- Answer sales objections and close more sales

- Utilize powerful telephone and marketing skills that will really work

- Increase your bottom line by developing other revenue streams

- Get to the real decision maker and quit wasting time

- Develop a memorable positioning statement that is key to your business

- Create marketing materials that will capture attention

- Identify the things you need to be doing to create a real business—not just go from speech to speech

These verbs focus on outcome language. This example comes from Henry DeVries, author of *Persuade with a Story*. They are perfect for a sales or marketing book:

- Improve lead generation

- Increase lead conversion rates

- Reduce wasted marketing

- Enable clients to maximize prices

- Help marketing departments exceed goals

BUILD YOUR BRAND WITH MNEMONIC LISTS

People who build the best personal brands often create their own language of memorable words, phrases, and sayings. Make your messages memorable—and repeatable—with mnemonic devices such as word lists and alliteration.

To create a mnemonic device, first create a word you want people to remember. Then use each letter to represent another word that shows action item you want people to do. The classic example is for goal-setting. If you want to create a great goal, it must be SMART, which stands for:

- Specific
- Measurable
- Attainable
- Relevant
- Time-based

Another useful technique is alliteration. That's the literary device in which each word starts with the same letter or sound. For example:

- From frugal to fruitful.
- Credibility and confidence create exciting outcomes.

Rhyming helps people remember your messages. Most people remember O. J. Simpson's defense attorney referring to the glove and saying, "If it doesn't fit, you must acquit."

CHECKLISTS

A checklist is a list of items you want readers to perform or a reminder of tasks to do. The boxes on a checklist add another interesting visual element. Readers get a sense of accomplishment when they mark off each completed item. You also can use checklists to promote your book in the form of handouts, bookmarks, and lead magnets.

Here's a checklist to write your book. I use this as a free offer, or a lead magnet, to get prospects to join my sales pipeline, so they can learn about this book and my services for book coaching, developmental editing, and ghostwriting. You can use an open circle or a blank box in front of each item, so people can check off their accomplishments.

Checklist for *Write Your Book in a Flash*

- Write executive summary
- Write back-cover copy
- Write Fool-Proof Positioning Statement

- Create title with a strong promise
- Write table of contents chapter themes (chapters 1–10)
- Outline each chapter with DESCRIBERS
- Research
- Write and edit the first draft
- Get feedback from peers and beta readers
- Revise
- Send the first draft to editor
- Publish the book
- Market the book

Ask yourself:

- Is it presented in order?
- Have you covered the important highlights?
- Did you cover each topic in enough depth?
- Did you include too much information that might bore readers?

You can download and print a copy of this checklist at
www.WriteYourBookInAFlash.com/worksheets

Flow Charts, Diagrams, and Process Visuals

Flow charts, diagrams, and process visuals illustrate processes. They show readers what happens step by step. They explain how things work. If you write a "how to" book, a visual is a wonderful way to outline and highlight the steps. Here is an example:

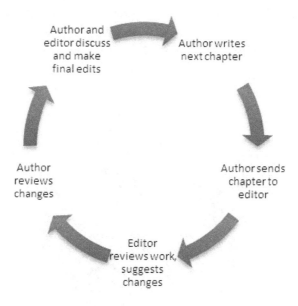

Figure 12: This flow chart shows a suggested work routine for an author and editor.

Visuals are easy to create if you have Microsoft Word, which calls them "SmartArt Graphics." Find them under the "Insert" tab on the menu.

You can choose from more than 75 fill-in-the-blank templates for lists, processes, cycles, hierarchies, relationships, matrices, and pyramids. Pick the ones you like, insert them into your manuscript, and fill in the blanks. You'll have professional-looking diagrams.

Readers who learn by seeing pictures instead of words will appreciate these graphics, which will help them better understand instructions and insights.

CHARTS AND GRAPHS

Numbers prove a point. Charts and graphs display those numbers in a style people can easily grasp. If you say 65 percent of people like to do something, 17 percent don't like to do something, and 18 percent are undecided, that's fine.

If you put a pie chart showing the same information, however, you'll make a more distinct impression, especially with people who process information better visually or who enjoy numbers. Scientists and marketers tend to love numbers.

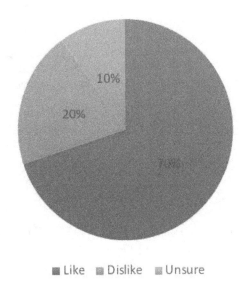

10%

20%

70%

■ Like   ■ Dislike   ■ Unsure

Figure 13: Charts and graphs help bring numbers to life and make your book more readable.

INFOGRAPHICS

An infographic is a visual representation of data. It can include a chart, diagram, or a process—or all of these in one visual element. In today's short-attention-span culture, infographics delight readers and get their attention. Plus, infographics break up long, dark walls of text.

Here's an infographic, courtesy of Venngage.com. If you want to create custom infographics, sign up for a free account with Venngage.com.

They offer hundreds of easy-to-use infographic templates to get you started.

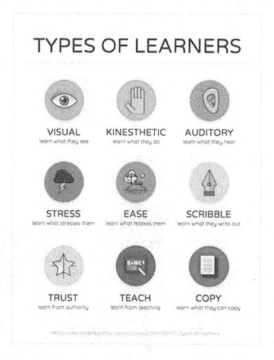

Figure 14: Infographics can bring a process to life by adding color and personality. Courtesy of Venngage.com

Pictures and Cartoons

A picture, they say, is worth a thousand words. Cartoons can add humor, which is always appreciated. Both graphic elements make your book more attractive and more accessible to readers.

You can draw stick figure cartoons. Or you can insert your pictures.

You can find pictures and cartoons online by searching for a KEYWORD and CARTOON (or PICTURE). For example, if you wanted a cartoon of a cat sleeping on a sofa, you'd go to Google and type "cartoon of cat sleeping on a sofa." It's that easy.

You can typically buy the rights to artists' works for a nominal fee. *Never* use a cartoon or picture without permission. I can't stress that strongly enough. If you use artwork without permission, you might—make that "probably *will*"—receive a threatening letter from a lawyer who will demand a great deal of money from you because you violated copyright law. Your lawyer (who you will also pay) will tell you to pay up.

There is no defense for stealing artwork, so pay the nominal fee upfront. Keep the bill of sale in case you need to prove your rights. Make sure you have bought the rights to use the artwork in a book, as opposed to online or in an ad. They might have different fees for each type of use. If you aren't sure, send them an email, and keep a copy of their response.

Figure 15: Jack Welch shares book marketing advice with Dan Janal. Photo by Wendy Blomseth.

SUBHEADS

Subheads are headings of subsections of a chapter. They break up the text and grab attention. They can be as simple as one word—as illustrated by the use of subheads here—or they can contain several words. They act as signposts to keep readers on track. My book-coaching clients who don't use subheads tend to have irrelevant information in sections. The minute they insert subheads, they can instantly see items that don't fit. It's amazing how a little subhead has such a powerful effect on readers and writers. Your outline contains ideas for your subheads.

Assignments and Exercises

Assignments and exercises perform several vital functions:

- Assignments add interactivity. People learn more by doing an assignment than when they merely read or hear information. When people see an assignment, they stop reading and start thinking about what the material means to them and how they can use it.

- Assignments can include blank lines or fill-in-the-blank lines, which add white space to make pages more attractive. For examples, refer to assignments throughout this book.

Summary/Highlights/Next Steps/Key Points/Lessons Learned

Summaries, highlights, next steps, key points, and lessons learned are texts appearing at the end of chapters. They do several important tasks:

- Summarize the chapter.

- Offer next steps.

- Preview the following chapter.

- Provide motivation.

Summaries reinforce your ideas and learning points. This follows the old strategy of "tell them what you will tell them, tell them, and then tell them what you told them."

Some people will read only the summaries as they skim through a book. Others use summaries as reminders when they reread or review the book.

Summaries or next steps can make the next chapter sound irresistible, so the reader turns the page to find more good information.

Many books don't use this device. You don't need to include a summary if you don't want to.

IF YOUR BOOK IS TOO SHORT

Your book needs to have at least 101 pages, so the spine is wide enough to print your name and title.

You can consider introducing these options if your book is a bit too short:

- Print blank pages at the end of each chapter. Better yet, print the word "Notes" on the top of those otherwise blank pages. People like to have room to take notes.

- Add blank pages at the end of the book.

- Add sales pages at the end of the book. Let people know services you offer.

- Add a longer bio. A short one is fine. If you need to fill pages, go into greater detail and add more elements on a second page. Don't use more than two pages.

- Print testimonials in larger type to fill more space. Put more white space between each testimonial.

NEXT STEPS

Design elements discussed in this chapter can make your pages look so interesting, your readers will not want to put the book down.

Next, we'll look at tools you can use to make the writing process easier.

CHAPTER 19

YOUR WRITER'S TOOL PALETTE

I write on big yellow legal pads—ideas in outline form when I'm doing stand-up and stuff. It's vivid that way. I can't type it into an iPad— I think that would put a filter into the process.

—Robin Williams

Many good tools can help you write your outline and book. Each person has their style, modality, or preference. You can decide which tool is best for you.

The best tools for creating an outline are:

- *Computer word processor*
- *Mind map*
- *Note cards*
- *Sticky notes*
- *Evernote*
- *Dictation*
- *Paper or journal*

Let's look at each tool.

COMPUTER WORD PROCESSOR

The word processor is my favorite, but don't let me bias you.

Every word processor has an outline function; however, you should spend five minutes to read the documentation or help file to learn how to use it properly. You'll find it has many features you hadn't thought of. Some key features are hard to find and difficult to use.

The outline tool will automatically track your outline structure. When you add a new thought, it adds a new letter or number. If you move an item, the word processor renumbers all items.

This will save you a lot of time as you create and update your outline. No doubt, you will move items dozens of times as you learn new ideas or decide to reorganize your ideas.

MIND MAP

A mind map is software that lets you visualize your ideas. If you are a visual person, this might make the most sense for you. I found I had to spend a lot of time learning how to use it. I was so frustrated and confused, I gave up. I was better off writing from an outline in a word processor; however, that's me. You might love mind maps.

STICKY NOTES

You can use sticky notes to arrange your notes and to create an outline. They come in different sizes and different colors, which can represent different subjects, so you can organize your ideas more easily. You will have to turn the handwritten notes into an outline on your computer.

INDEX CARDS, NOTE CARDS

Index cards, also called note cards, are old school. I remember using index cards in high school to write term papers. Believe me when I tell you they did *not* have computers when I was in high school. Looking back on those good old days, I must admit, there's something to be said for doing things the old-fashioned way.

First, when you use an index card, you write by hand. You might create different ideas and form different connections if you put pen to paper rather than type on a computer.

The other advantage is the writing space is big enough to explore one idea, but too small to add a second idea. Frankly, in that simplicity lies the beauty of note cards. You are forced to be concise, and you must limit your ideas to one key thought. Since only one idea is on a card, you can easily sort the cards, and move ideas around without having a second idea hitchhiked onto your card. I'll resist obvious parallels to Twitter, but there is elegance to a single idea in a single tweet. #Organized.

In addition to the key thought, you should write the publication source, author, page number, or link and title of the book or article. This will help you if you include a resources section or if you need to check your sources.

As with sticky notes, there is no downside, but you will have to eventually type your notes into an outline on your computer.

SCRIVENER

Many writers love Scrivener. It is a word processor, outline tool, note pad, and (as they say on TV) much, much more. Think of it as a word processor on steroids. My favorite feature lets you convert your book into many file formats for e-book publishing.

It has a significant learning curve, so be prepared to invest a few hours to get the most out of the product. However, a regular word processor might be all you need. It is reasonably priced at less than $50.

EVERNOTE

Evernote is a note-taking program and app, not a word processor. You type or speak your ideas into Evernote. Also, you can paste pictures and copy text from web pages. The free version provides all the power you need.

DICTATION

You can dictate ideas and notes into your phone or computer. I've been impressed with the speech-to-text recognition system on my iPhone. It is amazingly accurate.

Journal or Legal Pad

If words flow easily from your pen or pencil, then follow your muse. Business coach Evan Bulmer wrote *The Numbers that Matter* on a legal pad. Be prepared to transfer your work to a computer. There isn't an agent or book acquisitions editor in the United States who will accept a book, outline, or proposal on a legal pad.

Next Steps

The best tool is the one you find easiest to use. What works for me might not work for you and vice versa. That's the beauty of having so many tools to choose from.

Writing has been called "a lonely profession," but help is available. The next section shows how to collaborate with coauthors, coaches, and developmental editors.

SECTION IV. FINISHING TOUCHES FOR YOUR BOOK

CHAPTER 20

YOU DON'T HAVE TO DO IT ALL YOURSELF

Coaching isn't therapy. It's product development, with you as the product.

—Fast Company (magazine)

Writing should be fun. If it isn't, you should hire a ghostwriter or a book coach.

Let's not beat around the bush: If you don't like to write or think you can't write, you shouldn't torture yourself into thinking you have to be the one to write your book. If you know you can't or just won't write your book, it's time to get help instead of being miserable and never finishing the job. Sorry, but I think you'd rather hear the truth, take appropriate steps to leverage your knowledge, and gain your fame without worrying yourself to death.

There's no rule saying you have to write your book by yourself. In fact, many books are collaborations between you—the executive or thought leader writer—and a helper, such as a developmental editor, a book coach, a designer, a copy editor, a ghostwriter, or a coauthor.

Ken Blanchard, author of *The One-Minute Manager* and 60 other books that have sold more than 20 million copies total, told me he prefers working with a coauthor because they can learn from each other. Doesn't that put a positive reframe on collaborating?

Figure 16: Ken Blanchard (left) told me that he likes to collaborate on books because he learns from his coauthors.

Luiz Zorzella, author of *Revenue Growth: Four Proven Strategies*, also told me he advocated having a coauthor. "Besides sharing the workload, it helped me tremendously get unstuck (different people get stuck in different things) and keep the pace (having an accountability partner with whom you need to discuss actual content, not just milestones)."

As a book coach and developmental editor, I've helped my clients find the right topics and content for their books. In one case, a seminar participant wanted to write a book about meetings and why they were horrible. I told him there were hundreds of books like that. Why not write a book that shows people how to overcome all the pesky problems that make meetings a big waste of time?

Another client wanted to write a guide and a workbook that would help nonprofits of every size write their strategic business plan. After we discussed the project, she realized that she should focus on a specific market segment and create one book, not two, to best meet her needs and their needs.

Which Writing Partner Do You Need?

Working with a collaborator begins with determining what level of support you need. Let's look at several options.

- Coach—helps keep you motivated and accountable. A coach can answer your questions or point you to resources. Before hiring a coach, ask yourself: Are you coachable? If you can ask questions, take direction, and do tasks, you are coachable. If you get defensive when people offer you constructive criticism, you probably are not coachable. Don't make your life—and the coach's life—miserable if you are not coachable.

- Ghostwriter—writes your book for you. They will interview you, review your notes, presentations, speeches, papers, and other content and turn it into a book. Ghostwriters could conduct original research. Ghostwriters may share byline credit with the expert, or they could be completely hidden from the public's view. You choose. Put the terms in the contract, so everyone understands their roles.

What Successful Thought Leaders Don't Want You to Know about Their Books

Would you like to know the dirty secret of many best-selling business authors?

They didn't write their books.

They hired a ghostwriter to write the book because their time is too valuable to write one. Writing a book takes many hours. These successful execs want to spend those hours making deals, flying to meetings, and spending quality time with their families, so they hire a ghostwriter.

Thought leaders who love to write could be too busy speaking at conferences, consulting at clients' headquarters, or networking to find their next jobs.

If that sounds like you, then hiring a writing partner like a ghostwriter or a book coach is a logical step for you to take.

You don't have to write your outline—or your book—by yourself. You could hire someone *like* me—or you could hire me.

How to Create a Great Working Relationship with Your Writing Partner

You can have a good relationship with your writing partner (coach, ghostwriter, editor) when you consider several issues at the beginning of the engagement.

Subject Matter Fit

Is this a good fit by topic?

The person doesn't need to be an expert in your field. That's your job; however, they should understand your key concepts and be interested in the subject. If your topic doesn't excite them, watch out. It's probably not a good fit.

A good writer can probably write about anything, as I proved in my newspaper days when I wrote about cops, courts, schools, and human interest *all on the same day.* It's the ghostwriter's job to take your words and make them shine.

Personality Fit

Do you get along with each other? If not, then don't hire them.

Just as a bad shoe doesn't feel better over time, a bad personality fit will not get better either. If you like to hear comments without any sugarcoating, don't hire a touchy-feely person who is indirect. If you like to get started with small talk, don't hire a coach who gets right to point when you prefer talking about what you did over the weekend.

Can you communicate easily with the writer? Does it feel like you are talking to a friend, a student, or a partner? That's great. Does it feel like you are talking to a prosecutor, a debater, or a detractor? That might not be a good fit—unless you like being challenged.

Work Style Fit

Are your work styles compatible?

Everyone has a different work style and communication style.

What works best for you? Here's an exercise I read about in Pat Flynn's book **Will It Fly?** Think of three bosses or coworkers you liked. Now think of the reasons you liked them. Answers could be: They gave me clear goals. They showed me how to improve my work and made it seem easy. They sent me emails, which I liked better than meeting face to face.

Now think of three people you didn't like to work with. List the reasons why it was a bad fit. For example, they didn't tell me "why" I should do something. They sent me memos, but I preferred talking things through. They told stories, but I preferred direct messages, not beating around the bush.

After you do this exercise, you'll realize the kinds of people who motivate you and their style, as well as the kinds of people who burn you out.

The examples of "good" and "bad" vary by person. What turns one person on might turn another person off. It's important to know what works for you, so you can have a productive relationship without stress.

Your Turn: Best and Worst Bosses

Write three examples of bosses/coworkers you liked and why you liked them:

1._____

2. _____

3. _____

Write examples of bosses/coworkers you hated and why:

1. _____

2. _____

3. _____

WHAT ARE YOUR BOUNDARIES?

People don't think about setting boundaries when they begin business relationships. For example, clients who expect feedback at a certain time—but don't say so upfront—will be disappointed when their coach responds after a time the client considers too late. Perhaps you'd like feedback within 24 hours. Sounds good. But what if you send the material to the coach at 8:00 p.m. Friday, and the coach gets back to you on Monday? Is that acceptable? Or will you blow a gasket? To avoid any misunderstanding, I suggest defining and agreeing to these terms in the beginning. Mismatched expectations or definitions can ruin the relationship.

FINANCIAL CONSIDERATIONS

Write all terms and responsibilities, to avoid any confusion. Don't rely on your memory. A formal contract written by lawyers or a simple letter of understanding should state such terms as:

- What each person will do
- When they will do it
- Payment terms
- The due dates of drafts and final manuscript
- Delivery terms
- Terms of acceptance

NEXT STEPS

You don't have to do it all to get it all. Coaches, writers, and editors can help you produce every aspect of your book.

We're ready to finish the book!

CHAPTER 21

FINAL STROKES—PUTTING IT ALL TOGETHER

In soloing—as in other activities—
it is far easier to start something than it is to finish it.

—Amelia Earhart

When do you know you are finished?

If you've followed the steps, you should be done. Send the book to your publisher and see what they think.

THE ART OF THE FINISH

Anyone can start a book. Fewer people can finish a book. In fact, upward of 80 percent of people who start a book never finish. Let's make sure you are not one of those people who see a book by their competitor and say, "I could have written that." Or, "I could write something better than that."

FINAL WORDS OF INSPIRATION

One of my publicity clients, Roberta Matuson, offers this final word of advice: "If you don't write this book, someone else will write it, and you'll be upset. You'll say, 'Who wrote my book? How did I let that happen?'"

Two other final thoughts to keep you writing:

- Where would the world be if you didn't write your book?
- Where will your career be if you do write the book?

Summary

Congratulations! You now have all the tools, instructions, and inspiration you need to tell your story.

Whether you want to change the world or change your bank account, I'm here to help you. Please send me links to your finished books. I'd love to see how you've taken these ideas and turned them into books you are proud of. Please send me your comments. I'd like to know what you found useful and what you think can be improved. Ask me anything: dan@prleads.com

Good luck!

ACKNOWLEDGMENTS

Thanks to my clients—thousands of thought leaders, coaches, consultants, authors, and speakers—who have taught me so much.

Special thanks to my beta readers for offering invaluable advice and support: Margo O'Dell, Rhonda Gilliland, Louise Griffin, Heidi Pozzo, Rob Oliver, Cathy Paper, Kevin Donlin, Stephen Moulton, Melissa Wilson, Anita Mahaffey and Kelly Vreizen. Jill Noelle-Nobel for editing.

Thanks to these authors who generously shared their ideas: Henry DeVries, David A. Fields, Henry Juntilla, Amy Jauman, David Horsager, Michael Hauge, Pat Flynn, Sam Horn, and Cheri Grimm.

Thanks to my NSA-Minnesota pals for sponsoring my seminar and letting me test ideas: Jeff Ferrazzo and Kristin Brown.

Thanks to my marketing genius, Adam Hommey.

Thanks to my publisher, Tom Corson-Knowles and the team at TCK Publishing. It takes a village to sell books.

How to Work with Dan Janal as Your Coauthor, Developmental Editor, or Book Coach

> "Working with Dan has been like a master class in book writing. He is much more than a writing coach—he is a muse, teacher and friend, who makes the process enjoyable. This has been a great learning experience. I could not make this book happen without his expertise and support."
>
> —Alan Cohen, executive coach, author, *The Connection Challenge: How Executives Create Power and Possibility in the Age of Distraction*

Every professional athlete has a coach. Many CEOs have coaches. Shouldn't you have a coach for your book?

The following pages describe my services in detail.

To see if we're a good fit, I invite you to take a free, 20-minute, no obligation

"Assessment Coaching Session" with me. You'll get clear on:

- Your goals
- Your assets
- What's holding you back
- How people like you have gone from where you are to where you want to go
- How to get started

Schedule your appointment for your free, no-obligation, Assessment Coaching Session with me. Click this link, or type it into your browser: **www.WriteYourBookInAFlash.com/coaching**

I'm looking forward to helping you.

Dan Janal's Coaching Programs and Writing/Developmental Editing Services

I have several writing and coaching programs so you can get the feedback, encouragement, guidance, and support you need. There's a program for every budget. Here are several options:

I. Coaching Programs

Gold Coaching Program—You and I work on a structured coaching program that helps you create your executive summary and short summary, your Fool-Proof Positioning Statement, the title for your book, and the outline for the book, chapter by chapter. We discuss how to get testimonials, create stories, and conduct research. This coaching program is 10 sessions long and can be completed as quickly as you like—in as little as 10 days or 10 weeks (recommended). If your schedule requires more time, that's fine. The schedule is flexible to meet your needs.

Silver Coaching Program—I'll provide you with accountability, feedback, and brainstorming. You write your book, and I'll review it. If you don't write, I'll kick your butt. Packages of 12 weeks each are available.

II. Editorial and Writing Services

1. Developmental editing—I won't write your book. I'll give you direction for your book, review your work as you write, and provide feedback. You'll get the best possible book you wanted to write.

2. Editorial Book Packaging—For authors who have extensive written materials (i.e., blogs, articles, speeches, or transcripts from podcasts and webcasts), I'll review all your content, create an outline, and edit your works to fit inside a book. You can write new material, if needed, but the majority of the book already will have been contained in your intellectual property. I can create your book in about two months. This estimate is based on the quality and quantity of your materials and my other time commitments.

3. Ghostwriting—I'll write your book from scratch. This is the most full-service offering. Timing is based on an individual basis. Pricing is based on how much material you have created and how much material needs to be created.

4. Outlining. You and I will collaborate to write the outline of your book. The outline is a gigantic operational plan for your book. You could write the book from this outline. Or you can give the outline to your ghostwriter, who can follow our instructions. The average time to complete this outline is 10 hours.

For information, go to *WriteYourBookInAFlash.com*

WORKSHOP: WRITE YOUR BOOK IN A FLASH

Do you want to know the secret to writing a book without wasting time or money?

"Write a Book in a Flash" shows thought leaders, business executives, and entrepreneurs how to get focused fast and write your book without tearing your hair out. Most people dream of writing books, but they never complete the book. They have too many ideas or not enough ideas. Simply put, they aren't organized.

You'll discover:

- How to write a comprehensive outline that keeps you focused—and have fun doing it

- How to get stunning testimonials that can help sell your book

- How to overcome "The Imposter Syndrome" and other limiting beliefs that stifle nearly every person who ever wanted to write a book

- Clear examples that show you what to do

- Empowering exercises that show you how to write better and faster

- Simple how-to steps that anyone can follow

Even if you hate writing, you'll feel good about writing your book. Most importantly, you'll get the job done.

This is the perfect seminar to attend if you want to write a business book that builds your personal brand, opens doors to new opportunities, and leaves a legacy of business wisdom to future generations. Executives, entrepreneurs, coaches, consultants, and speakers who write books all get more clients, charge higher fees, have more impact, and develop a greater sense of worth. Let's get started now.

Unlike other seminars on writing a book, "Write Your Book in a Flash" doesn't teach grammar or debate the pros and cons of self-publishing vs. traditional publishing. Instead, it shows you how to use your own work style and personal quirks so you can write the book you were meant to share with the world.

Dan Janal has written six books for Wiley and has self-published three others. He is an award-winning daily newspaper reporter and business newspaper editor. He interviewed President Gerald Ford and First Lady Barbara Bush. Dan earned bachelor's and master's degrees in journalism from Northwestern University's famed Medill School of Journalism.

Next Steps:

1. Bring the "Write Your Book in a Flash Workshop" to your group. Email **dan@prleads.com** for details.

2. Attend a webinar based on "Write Your Book in a Flash." Click this link to see dates: **www.WriteYourBookInAFlash.com/webinars**

3. Hire Dan Janal to be your book coach or ghostwriter, or speak at your event. Email Dan at: **dan@prleads.com**

"Writing a book can be a really daunting endeavor. Dan Janal streamlines the book writing process for people who have great ideas, experiences, and stories, but need a true partner to bring all of those ideas into book form (without going crazy along the way). I've been fortunate enough to use Dan's wide variety of services, and I've found great value in each of them. I began as a PR LEADS subscriber, attended several of Dan's webinars, have read his new book, and I'm a current coaching client. I feel so lucky to have Dan on my side, helping me to fulfill my goal of writing my first book!"

—Stephanie Blackburn Freeth, founder, Adaptive Alternatives LLC, author, *The Nonprofit Strategy Tango: I Lead, You Follow and Together We Create Your Next Strategic Plan*

Podcasts and Webinars with Dan Janal

I love doing webinars and podcasts! I'd be happy to appear on your program. Each session helps your listeners:

- Write your book in a flash (Focus: outline)

- Never run out of ideas for your book (Focus: research)

- Ten tips to finish your book (Focus: overcome limiting beliefs)

- Get testimonials, beta readers, and reviewers for your book

- Your ideas. Dan is open to discussing your topics

To schedule a date and discuss topics, please select a time on Dan's schedule app: **www.WriteYourBookInAFlash.com/schedule**

Book Discounts and Special Deals

Sign up for free to get discounts and
special deals on our best-selling books at

www.TCKPublishing.com/bookdeals

ABOUT THE AUTHOR

Photo by Jen Kelly, Kelicomm

Dan Janal has written more than a dozen books to help businesses build their brands. Six have been translated into other languages. He is an award-winning daily newspaper reporter and business newspaper editor. As a publicity and marketing expert, he has helped more than ten thousand authors and experts build their platforms over the past seventeen years with his highly regarded PR LEADS services. He holds bachelor's and master's degrees in journalism from Northwestern University's famed Medill School of Journalism.

When Dan helps thought leaders and business executives write their books, either as a ghostwriter or as a book coach, he helps them take their businesses to the next level and exert greater influence. You can reach him at dan@prleads.com or

www.WriteYourBookInAFlash.com

Dan Janal is considered one of the founding fathers of Internet marketing because he wrote one of the first books on the field way back in 1993. The *Los Angeles Times* called Dan "an Internet marketing expert."

As a reporter, he interviewed President Gerald Ford and First Lady Barbara Bush. He was on the PR team that launched AOL.

He lives with his wife and two cats in a lakeside house in Minnesota and in a condo overlooking the Pacific Ocean near San Diego.

Books by Dan Janal

Write Your Book in a Flash!

Reporters Are Looking for YOU!

Internet Marketing Confidential

Business Speak

Risky Business

101 Successful Businesses You Can Start on the Internet

101 Businesses You Can Start on the Internet

Dan Janal's Guide to Marketing on the Internet

Internet Marketing Handbook (1988 edition)

Internet Marketing Handbook (1987 edition)

Internet Marketing Handbook

Publicity Builder (software)

How to Publicize High Tech Products and Services

CONNECT WITH DAN ON SOCIAL MEDIA

LinkedIn: **www.WriteYourBookInAFlash.com/linkedin**

Facebook: **www.WriteYourBookInAFlash.com/facebook**

Twitter: **www.WriteYourBookInAFlash.com/twitter**

Facebook group for "Write Your Book in a Flash!"
www.WriteYourBookInAFlash.com/community

APPENDIX/SELECTED RESOURCES

Books on Writing

The War of Art, by Steven Pressfield

Bird by Bird, by Anne Lamott

The Dip, by Seth Godin

On Writing, by Stephen King

2k to 10k: Writing Faster, Writing Better, and Writing More of What You Love, by Rachel Aaron

Pop! Create the Perfect Pitch, Title, or Tag Line for Anything, by Sam Horn

Marketing with a Book: The Science of Attracting High-Paying Clients for Consultants and Coaches, by Henry DeVries

Persuade with a Story, by Henry DeVries

Proposals that Sell, by Terry Whalin

For a free checklist for your book proposal, go to

terrylinks.com/bookcheck

Online Courses

How to Become a Best-Selling Author on Amazon Kindle, by Tom Corson-Knowles

Presenter Media—offers hundreds of professionally designed templates for presentations. I used them in this book as well as in webinars and in-person seminars.